# health food
# COOKERY

## Marguerite Patten

Hamlyn
London · New York · Sydney · Toronto

# CONTENTS

Published by
The Hamlyn Publishing Group Limited
London · New York · Sydney · Toronto
Hamlyn House, Feltham, Middlesex, England
© Copyright 1972 The Hamlyn Publishing Group Ltd.
ISBN 0 600 34371 5
Printed in England by Cox & Wyman, Ltd., Fakenham

The author and publishers gratefully acknowledge
the help of the following companies, who have
kindly provided the colour photographs as shown:

**British Egg Information Service**
Eggs in browned butter, page 51
Omelette, page 51
**'Carmel' Agrexco (Agricultural
Export Co. Limited of Israel)**
Apple and avocado salad and
avocado honey ice, page 23
Ogen baskets, page 31
**Pasta Foods Ltd.**
Wholemeal pasta rings, page 55
**Spong & Co. Ltd.**
Cucumber and orange salad, page 19

Cover photograph by John Lee

Dishes and accessories used in the photographs
kindly loaned by:
David Mellor (Ironmonger), 4 Sloane Square, London S.W.1
Casa Pupo, 60 Pimlico Road, London S.W.1
Whitefriars Glass Limited

# INTRODUCTION

There is no more priceless possession than good health; by that I do not mean an absence of complaints, but the feeling of *true* health, which gives boundless energy and a real enjoyment in living.

Many things contribute to good health—family and personal happiness, pleasant surroundings, a sensible balance between work and leisure and good food.

There are misconceptions about the meaning of 'good' food—to some people it signifies luxurious and exotic dishes; to others 'plain straightforward' meals. Both these groups of people are *right*—good food basically is the food you *enjoy*, but in planning ideal menus for enjoyment it is wise, and quite easy, to select the nutritious foods which give scope for imaginative cooking—and which can, and will, play a major part in keeping you and your family healthy.

Lack of time often encourages us to buy 'convenience' (canned, pre-packed, frozen) foods. These have a place in our busy modern existence but are meant to be used in conjunction with fresh foods, not as a complete alternative.

One of the problems in our ultra-civilised existence is that a high percentage of the population, children as well as adults, are overweight. In most cases this is through eating too much food or the *wrong* kind of food.

This book is *not* a book of slimming diets, it is a book giving recipes and menus of *enjoyable* meals made from the natural foods that are readily available, and which provide the nutrients we need for health-giving meals.

In order that you may assess the value of individual dishes in a sensible slimming routine, each recipe carries a 'star' marking.

❀❀❀ Low in calories—can be eaten in generous quantities.

❀❀ Be more sparing with portion if you wish to lose weight.

❀ One small portion if you are on a fairly strict diet.

I would like to thank Winifred Hoey, of the Hamlyn Group, for her help and encouragement in writing this book.

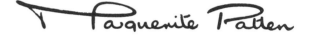

# EQUIPMENT TO HELP YOU

Although the equipment suggested is certainly *not* essential for producing the recipes in this book, it is extremely helpful.

## Slicer and shredder

The salad recipes, starting page 16, frequently mention shredded cabbage, sliced beetroot and other vegetables, etc. While these can be prepared by hand, it is appreciably quicker to use an appliance, and means the food is fresher looking when served. A hand-operated model, as illustrated, is both efficient and inexpensive.

## A liquidiser (blender)

Nothing is more warming than a good home-made soup of freshly cooked vegetables, herbs, etc. It takes a matter of seconds to purée the vegetables and produce a soup.

The liquidiser can prepare purées of fruit, etc., for sauces and desserts.

It can also 'chop' some of the ingredients for dressings, salads, stuffings, etc.

In some recipes, e.g. soups, page 10, it is suggested that vegetables are 'dropped' through the 'hole' left by removing the cap in the lid. If your particular liquidiser does not have such a lid, then make a round of foil, sufficiently large to put right over the top of the goblet, and cut a round 'hole' in this.

## Juice separator

Fresh fruit and vegetable juices are not only refreshing but health-giving too. A juice separator enables you to extract the juice from firm fruits—apples, etc., and such important vegetables and herbs as carrots, parsley, etc.

## Mincer

A hand mincer, or mincing attachment on an electric mixer is invaluable for grinding nuts and other ingredients.

## Grater

There are various ways in which one can grate cheese, vegetables, etc. Illustrated are two varying types.

# THE EFFECT OF FOODS ON HEALTH

All too often the effect of various foods is not appreciated and I would like to outline briefly some of the most essential foods and the reasons WHY they are so important. It has been said that our bodies are the 'foods we eat' and this is true.

## Proteins

While, to many people, the ONLY proteins worth considering are meat, fish and poultry, to others these are the proteins they do NOT wish to eat. Whatever one's personal opinion the inescapable facts are as follows.

We *need proteins* to build up healthy body tissue as we grow, and to maintain this when adult, *but* we can obtain protein from many foods—let me list the most important: meat, poultry, fish, cheese, eggs, nuts, milk, soya beans, the pulses (peas, beans, lentils), the seeds (sesame, etc.), the grains (wheat germ, brown rice, etc.), some fruits and vegetables (avocado pears, sprouts, are good examples).

As there are so many books giving recipes and suggestions for cooking and serving meat, poultry and fish, I have omitted recipes using them in this book. Many of you will not be surprised, as you will have planned your menus for some years without these particular protein

foods—to others of you may I suggest you try a *change of proteins*, you may well save money and I am sure you will enjoy the results.

## Carbohydrates

Over the past years this word has become the symbol of the foods one should NOT eat. This is nonsense—we need wholesome carbohydrates to create energy. It is an 'over-dose' of carbohydrates, to the exclusion of foods providing proteins, vitamins, mineral salts, etc., which is so bad. Let me list some of the health-giving carbohydrates one should include:

### Starches

*Flour:* this book deals with using wholemeal (stoneground) flour for baking. The wheat germ not only provides starch, it gives protein and vitamin B, discussed on page 8. Wholemeal pasta and brown rice are the basis of excellent meals (see pages 38, 52).

*Starchy vegetables:* peas and beans also provide proteins so should be included in the diet. Potatoes (particularly when new) add essential vitamin C (see page 8) to the diet.

### Sugars

*Sugar* itself is the basis of so many preserves, etc. Wherever possible I have used unrefined brown sugar, for, like honey and black treacle (a source of iron), this is an important health-giving 'sweetener'.

Remember many fruits and some vegetables (carrots for example) contain natural sugars.

The golden rule is to eat carbohydrates in limited amounts if your weight is normal, but to cut down on these if you need to lose weight.

## Fats

A reasonable amount of fat is needed by the body to create a feeling of warmth. If you follow a vegetarian diet then you will not have this fat from meat, or perhaps, butter, but you can replace it with the oils from nuts, corn or sunflower seed oil, etc., and from margarine.

There are two distinct 'schools of thought' about omitting fat from a slimming diet. Many diets cut fats to an absolute minimum, other diets stress that a certain amount of fat helps to 'burn up' the carbohydrates. Medical opinion is also divided upon whether animal fats, by increasing the cholesterol level in the body, are harmful. Too high a cholesterol is often blamed for hardening of the arteries and heart troubles, although modern opinion now tends to feel that sugars and starches, eaten to excess, are probably more harmful.

If, therefore, you are worried about eating animal fats, the solution is simple—just change over to the vegetable oils and vegetarian fats.

## Some important 'extras'

Before considering the effect of various minerals and vitamins upon your health (see pages 7 and 8), it is necessary to appreciate that each person varies in the amount of these required. Some of you may well find you obtain sufficient from the foods you eat; other people in the family, eating the same foods, could suffer from a deficiency. Remember that you can obtain tablets, etc., that provide both minerals and vitamins, from Health Food Stores and some chemists.

If you have not followed a natural food plan of eating before, you may be mystified by the importance given to certain foods, etc. I have therefore outlined their value below:

**Apple cider vinegar**—a natural acid that contains most minerals. It helps to correct overweight, invigorates the kidneys, etc.

**Bone meal**—bone meal tablets provide some of the most essential minerals, i.e. calcium, phosphorous and iron in particular. Bone meal is prepared from powdered bones of young beef cattle, so is a natural product.

**Brewer's yeast**—is the most effective natural yeast, which adds an appreciable amount of protein to the diet, as well as helpful carbohydrates, fats, minerals and vitamins (the vitamin B-complex in particular). Brewer's yeast may be added to food in cooking.

**Honey**—this is one of the most perfect natural foods, as well as being a pleasant form of sugar, which gives almost instant energy.

**Muesli**—this interesting blending of natural foods is described on page 36, it can be obtained ready-prepared in Health Food Stores.

**Treacle**—(molasses)—black treacle is a splendid source of iron and other minerals, etc. Use it when possible.

**Yoghourt**—one of the most easily digested of foods; low in calories, high in food value. It is an excellent source of calcium; it also provides protein, some fat, carbohydrate and vitamins. It is possible to make your own yoghourt (see page 58). Natural yoghourt is the lowest in calories.

# Minerals

Listed on this page are some of the most important minerals. I am not enlarging on all minerals present in food, or all those needed by the body. These 'trace' minerals all have an important part to play in ensuring healthy growth, the maintenance of a strong constitution and mental vigour.

Often it is said that a 'normal' well balanced diet will make certain you have these minerals. That is true, providing you check that yours *is a well balanced diet*. By that I mean a diet rich in proteins (including whole grains—wheat germ in particular), a generous amount of fresh vegetables and fresh fruit. In addition, regular amounts of honey, treacle (molasses), bone meal and brewer's yeast also help, see the opposite page.

**Calcium**—this essential mineral helps to give strong bones, good teeth, aids circulation and helps to avoid premature ageing. It is needed by all ages. Obviously especially by children as they grow, to keep their bones and teeth healthy (although dental decay can be due to too many sweet foods and inadequate dental care). Pregnant women and nursing mothers need extra calcium; the elderly must have good supplies to prevent their bones becoming ultra-brittle and breaking easily.

Calcium is in most fresh foods, cheese, milk and milk products in particular (some indication is given that pasteurisation of milk has an adverse effect upon calcium content). You will also obtain calcium from whole grains, honey, treacle, soya beans, poultry, meat, fish, nuts, some vegetables (potatoes, sprouts, broccoli in particular) and fresh fruit.

**Phosphorus**—I have listed this next to calcium for, like calcium, it is necessary for the formation of good teeth and bones. It also assists in the digestion of carbohydrates and fats. It must be remembered that vitamin D helps the body to absorb both calcium and phosphorus, so check you have adequate supplies of this (see page 8).

Phosphorus is present in egg yolk, fish, meats (particularly liver and kidney), in milk, cheese, nuts. Nearly all fruits and vegetables contain a certain amount of phosphorus. Cranberries in particular provide phosphorus, so do red cabbage and beetroot tops.

**Iron**—ensures healthy red blood. A severe lack of iron causes anaemia. Iron deficiency can produce dull-looking hair, early skin wrinkling, sore gums, brittle finger nails and a tired listless feeling. We all need iron, particularly women, who lose blood at monthly periods, and expectant or nursing mothers.

Vitamin C (see page 8) helps the body absorb iron.

Iron is present in beef, liver, kidneys, heart, in turkey, egg yolk, whole grains, honey, black treacle (molasses), wheat germ (in flour), cocoa, the dark green vegetables (parsley, spinach, watercress) and dried fruit such as apricots and prunes, also peanuts.

**Chlorine**—its main purpose is to aid the removal of toxic products from the body.

It is present in milk and milk products, leafy green vegetables and uncooked meat.

**Copper**—this aids the body to assimilate iron. A serious lack of copper though can impair breathing.

Copper is in egg yolk, liver, black treacle (molasses), green vegetables, whole grains, soya flour and apricots, figs and prunes.

**Fluorine**—helps to decrease dental decay (if other principles of dental care are followed). An excessive amount causes white marks on teeth.

It is found in varying degrees in drinking water, to a less degree in fish and other foods. There is some controversy as to whether it should be added to the drinking water where not present naturally.

**Iodine**—the body needs very little of this mineral, but that small amount is essential to life. It helps relieve nervous tensions and is important to control the proper functioning of the thyroid gland.

It is present in certain fish (haddock, cod, cod-liver, salmon, lobster, oysters). It is also available in seaweeds, in milk and milk products, and in some vegetables, particularly onions and in bananas, strawberries and peanuts.

**Sodium chloride**—(salt)—is necessary to prevent cramp, although some people have to reduce the amount of salt in their diet (due to too high blood pressure).

This is present in the body fluid, and is added to foods (natural sea salts are obtained from ocean plant life).

## A look at some vitamins

Vitamins have been described as 'protective elements' in food. They are not foods themselves and one could not live on a diet of vitamins alone, but they are essential to good health and a feeling of vitality. As you will see, they come from fresh foods and some of them can be lost when the food becomes stale.

**Vitamin A**—is essential for a clear skin and healthy looking eyes. A severe deficiency could cause 'night blindness', i.e. an inability to adjust from light to darkness. Vitamin A helps to assist healthy growth, protects the linings of the nose, mouth, ears, aids digestion and is one of the essential vitamins to build-up resistance to infection, particularly of the prostate gland. Young children need extra vitamin A.

The best source of vitamin A is liver, fish liver oil, in fatty fish (such as herrings), egg yolk, butter, margarine, cheese, unskimmed milk, soya beans, carrots and green vegetables and some fruits.

**Vitamin B**—this is a complex group of vitamins, each member of the group playing a slightly different part in maintaining good health. They are essential for energy; a good digestion; for keeping the nervous system, eyes and skin healthy. B-vitamins allow the release of energy (the true value) from foods we eat. Some of the muscular diseases and sciatica, neuralgia, etc., are often helped by extra amounts of B-vitamins. A severe lack of these vitamins can cause, or accentuate, nervous disorders, insomnia and headaches. They cannot be stored in the body, so make sure you eat some of the foods that are rich in these vitamins each day.

The various vitamins in the B-complex are present in brewer's yeast, yeast extract, liver, heart and brains. Wheat germ is also one of the main sources, that is why when bread is omitted from a slimming diet you MUST choose other foods that will provide vitamin B to take its place. It is also sensible to add extra wheat germ to your normal diet. This group of vitamins are found, to a lesser degree, in peas, beans, soya beans, egg yolk, nuts, yoghourt and whole milk, brown rice and other seeds and some green vegetables. Vitamins of the B group can be destroyed in ultra-refined foods, this is why natural unrefined foods are so important.

**Vitamin C**—the best known of all, is sometimes known as ascorbic acid. The best known use of vitamin C is to ensure healthy skin, but it has many other values also. It helps to build up resistance to colds and virus, such as influenza, it helps to maintain healthy gums and aids the development of good teeth. Doses of extra vitamin C have been found very helpful to sufferers of asthma, hay fever, arthritis and muscular fatigue. Vitamin C helps in healing cuts and prevents (with calcium) brittle bones. One needs adequate supplies of vitamin C to allow the body to absorb iron. It cannot be stored in the body, so renew supplies daily.

Vitamin C is present in fresh natural foods, but rose hips, blackcurrants, citrus fruits, strawberries are the fruits richest in this vitamin, although most fruits will provide a certain amount. Potatoes, because we eat them regularly, are a valuable source, particularly when new and when cooked WITH the skin. Raw or lightly cooked green vegetables and tomatoes will provide this vitamin and so will sardines and soya beans.

**Vitamin D**—for good bone formation and good teeth. Vitamin D aids the body to absorb both calcium and phosphorus. A severe lack can cause rickets in young children and prevent the body using body-sugar properly, so one suffers from undue fatigue. The other values of this vitamin are to ensure eye health, regular heart action and, with vitamin K and calcium, to aid healthy blood clotting.

The main sources of vitamin D are in fish-liver oil (that is why halibut and cod-liver oil capsules are recommended), in oily fish, egg yolk, butter, margarine, whole milk and flower seeds. It is also absorbed into the body, through the skin, from sunlight.

**Vitamin E**—has a helpful effect on fertility and maintenance of healthy muscles.

It is in wheat germ, fresh vegetables and seeds.

**Vitamin F**—helps to maintain general good health, and the body to absorb calcium and vitamins A, D, E and K.

Vegetable oils and whole grains provide this vitamin.

**Vitamin K**—this, with calcium, ensures healthy blood clotting, so stops undue bleeding.

It is found in green leafy vegetables.

# GOOD BEGINNINGS

So you have decided to 'take a look' at a natural health food diet. As you will see there is nothing 'cranky' about it in any way. Health foods are good wholesome foods, that are full of flavour and give interesting and appetising meals.

If you are trying to cure minor ailments by a change of diet do not expect 'miracles', you must follow the diet and include the foods you feel should be helpful for a fair period of time.

When you wake in the morning with a few 'aches and pains' and a feeling of tiredness, try a mixture of apple cider vinegar and honey, or a glass of fresh lemon or orange juice, as a good morning 'cocktail'. Do this regularly and you WILL feel better.

Perhaps you have never been able 'to face' breakfast. Make the effort and have a protein dish, or a bowl of Muesli, as page 36. I am confident that you will feel far less tired as the morning goes on. Mid-morning fatigue is so often due to a poor breakfast or no breakfast. at all.

If you feel like a 'mid-morning nibble', try to avoid eating sweetmeats, a sticky bun or biscuits, and grab a crisp apple or carrot instead. Children, in particular, should be encouraged to develop this health-giving habit.

At first the children may resent having to alter familiar habits, but after a time I am sure they will begin to *like* the fresh natural taste and pleasant texture of the food you offer them. You will be helping them towards firm strong teeth and a liking for the right kind of food.

When you go shopping take a look at some of the less familiar foods—nuts and nut meat—that can give your family a delicious change.

If the housekeeping budget is low and you cannot afford as much meat, fish or poultry as you would wish, consider giving protein in a less familiar (and often less expensive) way. Look at the recipes using pulses or grains, pages 32 to 37. Decide to offer your family a larger variety of vegetables, served raw or lightly cooked or in a new dish. Remember raw or lightly cooked vegetables, like fresh fruit, not only supply food values, minerals and vitamins, but they ensure that the body has roughage to aid the process of good digestion and elimination of waste products.

Perhaps you pride yourself on your skill in baking cakes, etc? May I suggest you try baking with wholemeal (often called stoneground) flour. This flour retains all the natural value of the wheat germ, but just as important is the fact that it is the basis for the most delicious bread, so different from the all-too-familiar taste of the bulk-baking that we buy today. Wholemeal flour is just as interesting for brown pastry, cakes, etc. These will be a complete change for the family and a very real contribution to healthy living.

All too often we feel 'bored' with the familiar routines of eating, cooking, etc. I think it is both a pleasant challenge and change to take a look at the modern health foods and the new thoughts on health-giving meals, and to give them a really genuine trial.

# SOUPS

key to stars see page 5

You can capture the flavour of fresh vegetables in a delicious hot or cold soup. Remember you retain not only the delicious taste, but most of the valuable mineral salts, vitamin and food value as well. The shorter the cooking time, the better your soup will be.

A liquidiser (blender) is ideal for emulsifying the vegetables. Obviously in many cases you need to cook the vegetables with liquid (water, milk or stock), put the mixture into the goblet, switch on and leave until smooth, then serve. It saves a great deal of cooking time, and also retains more of the flavour of the food if the *raw* vegetables are emulsified with liquid.

If you wish to make a smooth purée, put the liquid and vegetables (cut in fairly small pieces) into the goblet, switch on and leave until ready. If you wish to have finely 'chopped' vegetables then put the liquid into the goblet, remove the cap from the lid or make a foil 'lid' with a 'hole' as suggested on page 4. Switch on and drop the vegetables through this, leave until evenly 'chopped'.

The vegetables are then ready to be heated for a short time, or served as a cold soup.

The only vegetable where I personally prefer the flavour if it is lightly cooked first, then put into the liquidiser, is a fairly large strong onion. Small onions are excellent used raw.

Mention is made above of using milk, this can be ordinary cows' or goats' milk, skimmed milk powder, or soya milk or plantmilk.

*Stock:* to make a good flavoured stock for making soups and other savoury dishes, blend yeast extract with water.

## Springtime vegetable soup ✳✳✳

| Imperial | American |
|---|---|
| small bunch spring onions | small bunch scallions |
| about 8 young carrots | about 8 young carrots |
| about 8 small new potatoes* | about 8 small new potatoes* |
| 1 small green pepper† | 1 small green pepper† |
| small young turnip | small young turnip |
| 1½ pints water | 4 cups water |
| little yeast extract | little yeast flavoring extract |

| to garnish | to garnish |
|---|---|
| chopped chervil | chopped chervil |
| chopped chives | chopped chives |

* leave skins on, if wished.
† remove core and most of the seeds; a few give a pleasant 'peppery' taste.

Wash all the vegetables very well. If possible leave the skins on. If using a liquidiser there is no need to chop the vegetables, just put a little of the water into the liquidiser, add the vegetables as suggested in the left-hand column, switch on and leave until fairly finely 'chopped'. If you have no liquidiser, dice the vegetables fairly finely. Put into a pan with the water and yeast extract. Bring to the boil and cook for a few minutes only, until the vegetables are just tender but not 'mushy'. Top with the chopped herbs. *Serves 4-6*

### To vary

*Summer soup:* ✳✳✳ add some fresh green peas, broad beans, few asparagus tips (if inexpensive). Omit the new potatoes. Garnish with chopped mint and chives, or to give a more delicate flavour, omit both of these and garnish with chopped dill or chopped fennel.

*Autumn soup:* ✳✳✳ use sliced green beans, pieces of celery, and substitute chopped larger onions in place of spring onions. Toss the chopped onions in a little corn oil to soften and give a milder flavour, then add to the other vegetables. Garnish with chopped chives mixed with a very little grated fresh horseradish.

*Winter soup:* ✳✳✳ use larger onions in place of spring onions, parsnip in place of new potatoes, add a little celery, and garnish the soup with chopped parsley, celery leaves and nuts, which add a pleasantly firm texture to the vegetables.

To make a meal in a bowl of soup, top with grated or cottage cheese.

## Chilled avocado soup ✾

| Imperial | American |
|---|---|
| 2 large ripe avocado pears | 2 large ripe avocado pears |
| 1 large lemon | 1 large lemon |
| ½ pint yoghourt | 1⅓ cups yogurt |
| 2 teaspoons honey | 2 teaspoons honey |
| 2-3 teaspoons corn oil | 2-3 teaspoons corn oil |
| pinch sea salt | pinch sea salt |

Do not halve the avocado pears until ready to make the soup. Halve, remove the pulp and either mash, then blend with the other ingredients, or put them all into the liquidiser. Serve very cold. Thin with a little more yoghourt or milk, if wished. *Serves 4-6*

## Apricot and cucumber soup ✾✾

| Imperial | American |
|---|---|
| 6 oz. dried apricots | ¾ cup dried apricots |
| 1 lemon | 1 lemon |
| 1½ pints water | 4 cups water |
| 2-3 teaspoons honey | 2-3 teaspoons honey |
| 1 large cucumber | 1 large cucumber |
| 1 medium onion | 1 medium onion |
| 1½-2 tablespoons sunflower seed or corn oil | 2 tablespoons sunflower seed or corn oil |
| 1-2 teaspoons curry powder | 1-2 teaspoons curry powder |
| little sea salt | little sea salt |

Put the dried apricots, with thin strips of lemon rind, to soak in the cold water overnight. Simmer gently in a pan with the lemon juice and honey until quite tender—this takes about 1 hour. Sieve or put the apricots and liquid into the liquidiser to make a smooth purée. Some of the lemon rind can be removed if wished. Cut a small piece from the cucumber to use for garnish. Peel the rest of the cucumber and the onion and chop finely. Toss for about 5 minutes in the oil, add the curry powder, the apricot purée and salt to taste. Simmer steadily for 10 minutes, then serve hot or cold, topped with thin strips of cucumber. This makes an excellent hot weather soup, and the contrast between the slightly sweet delicate curry flavour and the small pieces of cucumber and onion is delicious. *Serves 4-5*

### To vary

Omit the curry powder and blend a few tablespoons of yoghourt with the soup just before serving.

## Frosted cucumber mint soup ✾✾✾

| Imperial | American |
|---|---|
| 1 large cucumber | 1 large cucumber |
| 2 or 3 spring onions or chopped chives to taste | 2 or 3 scallions or chopped chives to taste |
| ½ pint yoghourt | 1⅓ cups yogurt |
| squeeze lemon juice | squeeze lemon juice |
| mint to taste | mint to taste |

Peel nearly all the cucumber; save a small unpeeled piece for garnish. Cut the cucumber and onions into pieces and put into the liquidiser with the other ingredients. Switch on until smooth.

Put into soup cups, and chill or put into the freezing compartment for a very short time. Garnish with twists of cucumber. *Serves 4-5*

### To vary

*Tomato and cucumber soup:* ✾✾✾ omit the mint and use parsley instead, and add 3-4 large skinned tomatoes.

This soup can be served hot, but heat very carefully so the mixture does not curdle. Top with chopped parsley and chopped chives. *Serves 4-6*

## Green pepper soup ✾✾✾

| Imperial | American |
|---|---|
| 2 medium green peppers | 2 medium green peppers |
| 2-3 large tomatoes | 2-3 large tomatoes |
| small piece cucumber | small piece cucumber |
| 1-2 cloves of garlic (optional) | 1-2 cloves of garlic (optional) |
| ¾ pint water | 2 cups water |
| 1-2 teaspoons yeast extract | 1-2 teaspoons yeast flavoring extract |
| 1-2 tablespoons chopped parsley | 1-2 tablespoons chopped parsley |

Remove the pulp from the peppers, discard the core and most of the seeds, but save a few to give a slightly 'peppery' taste. The tomatoes may be skinned if wished, but the skin should be kept on the cucumber. Crush the garlic.

Put the water and yeast extract into the liquidiser, then add the vegetables and 'chop' as suggested on page 10, column 1. If you do not wish to use a liquidiser, dice the vegetables neatly, mix with the garlic and the water blended with the yeast extract. Add the chopped parsley, serve very cold, or heat gently for about 10 minutes, so the vegetables retain an attractive firm texture. *Serves 4*

## Beetroot soup—hot ❁❁

| Imperial | American |
|---|---|
| 1 bunch young beetroot | 1 bunch young beets |
| 1 bunch spring onions or 2 onions | 1 bunch scallions or 2 onions |
| juice of 1 lemon or 1 tablespoon apple cider vinegar | juice of 1 lemon or 1 tablespoon apple cider vinegar |
| 2 pints water | $5\frac{1}{3}$ cups water |
| 1-2 teaspoons yeast extract | 1-2 teaspoons yeast flavoring extract |
| 2 teaspoons honey | 2 teaspoons honey |
| sea salt to taste | sea salt to taste |

| to garnish | to garnish |
|---|---|
| yoghourt | yogurt |
| chopped parsley | chopped parsley |

Wash the beetroot and onions well, and either grate the beetroot or put through a shredder or mincer. Chop or shred the onions. Put the lemon juice and water into the pan, bring to the boil, add the beetroot and onions, the yeast extract, honey and a very little salt. Simmer for about 35-40 minutes until the beetroot is quite soft. Top with yoghourt and parsley.     *Serves 4-6*

### To vary

*Tomato beetroot soup:* ❁❁ follow the directions above, but add 3-4 large chopped tomatoes with the beetroot and onions.

*Beetroot soup—cold:* ❁❁ add a small shredded sweet apple to the ingredients, and cook the soup as the recipe above. If wished you can boil a fairly large potato in its skin, remove the skin, mash the potato and add to the beetroot soup to thicken. Allow to cool, then top with yoghourt, chopped parsley and matchsticks of cucumber.

## Nuts in soup

Nuts may be added to many soups, either as a garnish or to give extra food value and a firm texture to the vegetables, etc. This chestnut soup is a well known classic soup and can be varied in many ways. Add other nuts—cashew or hazelnuts — to chestnuts (this produces a very delicious flavour). A more savoury soup is given by extra vegetables; a few tomatoes produce an interesting colour as well as flavour.

## Chestnut soup ❁❁

| Imperial | American |
|---|---|
| 1 lb. chestnuts | 1 lb. chestnuts |
| 1 pint water with 1-2 teaspoons yeast extract or use stock from boiling bacon or ham | $2\frac{2}{3}$ cups water with 1-2 teaspoons yeast flavoring extract or use stock from boiling ham |
| 2 oz. margarine | $\frac{1}{4}$ cup margarine |
| $\frac{1}{2}$ pint milk or use soya milk | $1\frac{3}{4}$ cups milk or use soy milk |
| seasoning (see method) | seasoning (see method) |

| to garnish | to garnish |
|---|---|
| 1-2 slices wholemeal bread | 1-2 slices wholewheat bread |

Split the skins of the chestnuts and boil in water for 10-15 minutes, until soft enough to skin. Do this while warm and keep the nuts in the water; it is much harder to skin them when they become cold. Put the peeled nuts back into a pan with the fresh water and yeast extract, or with the stock. Simmer for about 30-35 minutes until as soft as you like. The nuts are very pleasant if slightly firm, and while they are difficult to sieve they are excellent to put into the liquidiser. Put through a sieve with the stock, or into a warmed liquidiser goblet and switch on until smooth. Put back into the saucepan with the margarine, milk and seasoning if required.

I have omitted pepper, etc., from most soup recipes, for when using many fresh vegetables you may not wish to obscure their natural flavours with too much seasoning. Chestnuts though, have a very delicate flavour, so you may like to use sea salt or vegetable salt and a little pepper. Heat and serve topped with diced toasted bread.     *Serves 4-6*

### To vary

*Peanut soup:* ❁❁ use 8 oz. (1 cup) shelled peanuts instead of chestnuts.

## Clear mushroom soup ❊❊❊

| Imperial | American |
| --- | --- |
| 1-2 medium onions | 1-2 medium onions |
| 8 oz. mushrooms | 2 cups mushrooms |
| good 1 pint water | 3 cups water |
| 2 teaspoons brewer's yeast | 2 teaspoons brewer's yeast |

| **to garnish** | **to garnish** |
| --- | --- |
| 2 tablespoons chopped parsley | 2 tablespoons chopped parsley |

If using a liquidiser, simply peel and chop the onions coarsely and leave the washed mushrooms whole. If you are not using a liquidiser, then dice the onions and mushrooms quite finely. Put into a pan with the water and yeast. Simmer for about 10 minutes only. Taste, and add a little more brewer's yeast or yeast extract if wished. Serve very hot, topped with the chopped parsley.                    *Serves 4-5*

## Creamed mushroom soup ❊❊

| Imperial | American |
| --- | --- |
| 2 medium onions | 2 medium onions |
| 2 medium old potatoes | 2 medium old potatoes |
| 1½ tablespoons corn or sunflower seed oil | 2 tablespoons corn or sunflower seed oil |
| 1 clove of garlic (optional) | 1 clove of garlic (optional) |
| ½ pint water | 1⅓ cups water |
| 1-2 teaspoons yeast extract | 1-2 teaspoons yeast flavoring extract |
| 8 oz. mushrooms | 2 cups mushrooms |
| ½ pint milk or soya milk | 1⅓ cups milk or soy milk |
| sea salt to taste | sea salt to taste |

Peel the onions, and dice these with the well washed potatoes. Toss in the hot oil for a few minutes with the crushed garlic. Add the water and yeast extract, and simmer for about 15 minutes until the potatoes are fairly soft. Add the chopped mushrooms and milk, and cook for a further 5 minutes. Either sieve and reheat, or put into a warmed liquidiser. Add salt to taste.                    *Serves 4-6*

## Onion soup ❊❊❊

| Imperial | American |
| --- | --- |
| 4 medium onions | 4 medium onions |
| 1-2 cloves of garlic (optional) | 1-2 cloves of garlic (optional) |
| 1½ tablespoons corn oil | 2 tablespoons corn oil |
| 1½ pints beef stock or water and yeast extract | 4 cups beef stock or water and yeast flavoring extract |
| 1 slice wholemeal bread | 1 slice wholewheat bread |

| **to garnish** | **to garnish** |
| --- | --- |
| grated cheese | grated cheese |
| chopped parsley | chopped parsley |

Peel and cut the onions into thin rings. Crush the clove of garlic. Toss the onion rings and garlic in the hot oil until the onions are golden coloured. Add the stock, or water and yeast extract. Simmer steadily for about 30 minutes, then crumble the bread into the soup and stir until this has thickened it. Put into hot serving cups or dishes, and top with the cheese and parsley.                    *Serves 4-5*

## Potato and onion soup ❊

| Imperial | American |
| --- | --- |
| 3 medium onions | 3 medium onions |
| small piece celery root | small piece celery root |
| 4 medium potatoes | 4 medium potatoes |
| 1 clove of garlic | 1 clove of garlic |
| 1½ pints water | 4 cups water |
| 1 teaspoon yeast extract | 1 teaspoon yeast flavoring extract |
| ½-1 teaspoon sea salt | ½-1 teaspoon sea salt |
| 2-3 oz. cashew nuts | nearly ½ cup cashew nuts |

| **to garnish** | **to garnish** |
| --- | --- |
| chopped parsley | chopped parsley |
| chopped fresh tarragon | chopped fresh tarragon |

Peel and dice the onions, celery root and potatoes. Crush the clove of garlic. Put into a saucepan with the water, yeast extract and salt to taste. Simmer for 25 minutes, add the nuts, cook for a further 5 minutes. Sieve, or put into the warmed liquidiser goblet. Switch on until smooth. Heat if necessary and top with the chopped herbs. This is also excellent as a cold soup, topped with yoghourt and herbs.                    *Serves 5-6*

**To vary**

*Potato and leek soup:* ❊ use leeks instead of onions.

# Tomato soup ❋❋❋

| Imperial | American |
|---|---|
| 1 small onion | 1 small onion |
| small piece of celery (optional) | small piece of celery (optional) |
| small piece of apple | small piece of apple |
| 1 small uncooked beetroot | 1 small uncooked beet |
| 1 pint water | 2⅔ cups water |
| 1½ lb. ripe tomatoes | 1½ lb. ripe tomatoes |
| sea salt to taste | sea salt to taste |

| **to garnish** | **to garnish** |
|---|---|
| chopped parsley | chopped parsley |
| chopped lemon thyme | chopped lemon thyme |

Peel the onion. If you are using the liquidiser then chop coarsely, but if you do not wish to do this then shred the onion, celery, apple and beetroot neatly. Put into the boiling water and simmer for about 10 minutes. If you are not using a liquidiser, then chop the tomatoes neatly (skin if wished), and add to the vegetables. Just heat for a few minutes, adding salt to taste. If using a liquidiser, put the hot vegetables and liquid into the warmed goblet. Add the roughly chopped tomatoes (there is no need to skin them), switch on until smooth, then add salt to taste, and heat for a few minutes only. Serve topped with the herbs. *Serves 5-6*

## To vary:

*Cold tomato soup:* ❋❋ the recipe above gives a delicious cold soup. It can be topped with yoghourt or cottage cheese, and could be iced lightly.

## Serving iced or cold soups
Dip the rim of the soup cup into a little egg white, then in finely chopped parsley.

# Cheese and vegetable chowder ❋

| Imperial | American |
|---|---|
| 1 medium onion | 1 medium onion |
| 3 good sized carrots | 3 good sized carrots |
| small piece celery or celeriac (celery root) | small piece celery or celeriac (celery root) |
| small parsnip | small parsnip |
| 2 oz. peas | ½ cup peas |
| 2 oz. corn and/or 2 oz. sliced green beans | ½ cup corn and/or ½ cup sliced green beans |
| small piece of yam or sweet potato or 1 potato | small piece of yam or sweet potato or 1 potato |
| ½ pint water | 1⅓ cups water |
| ½-1 teaspoon yeast extract | ½-1 teaspoon yeast flavoring extract |
| 1-2 tablespoons chopped parsley | 1-2 tablespoons chopped parsley |
| ½-1 teaspoon chopped thyme | ½-1 teaspoon chopped thyme |
| ½-1 teaspoon chopped balm | ½-1 teaspoon chopped balm |
| 1-2 bay leaves | 1-2 bay leaves |
| 2 oz. margarine | ¼ cup margarine |
| 2 oz. wholemeal flour | ½ cup wholewheat flour |
| ¾ pint milk or soya or plantmilk | 2 cups milk or soy or plantmilk |
| pinch sea salt | pinch sea salt |
| pinch cayenne pepper | pinch cayenne pepper |
| 6 oz. grated Cheddar cheese | 1½ cups grated Cheddar cheese |

| **to garnish** | **to garnish** |
|---|---|
| paprika | paprika |
| chopped mixed herbs | chopped mixed herbs |

Peel the onion, wash and dice with the other vegetables. Remove the skin from the yam or sweet potato and other vegetables, if wished, although skins add so much flavour to the soup. Put the water and yeast extract into a pan, bring to the boil, then add the vegetables and herbs. Cook for approximately 15 minutes until the vegetables are just tender, but not over-soft. Remove the bay leaves. Meanwhile heat the margarine in a second good sized pan, stir in the flour and cook for 2-3 minutes over a low heat. Gradually blend in the type of milk you have chosen. Bring to the boil and cook until thickened. Add the salt and cayenne pepper (use this sparingly for it is very strong). Tip the cooked vegetables into the sauce, stir well then add the cheese. Heat for 2-3 minutes only, since over-cooking can spoil the texture of this soup, for the cheese becomes tough and could curdle. Put into hot soup cups, and top with the paprika and chopped herbs (choice of herbs is entirely personal). Omit cheese if preferred. *Serves 5-6*

# Lentil soup ✳✳

| Imperial | American |
|---|---|
| 8 oz. lentils | 1 cup lentils |
| 2 pints water | 5⅓ cups water |
| *bouquet garni** | *bouquet garni** |
| 1-2 teaspoons yeast extract | 1-2 teaspoons yeast flavoring extract |
| 2 medium onions | 2 medium onions |
| 2-3 medium carrots | 2-3 medium carrots |
| several sticks celery | several sticks celery |
| sea salt to taste | sea salt to taste |
| good pinch paprika or curry powder | good pinch paprika or curry powder |

| **to garnish** | **to garnish** |
|---|---|
| chopped chives and/or chopped parsley | chopped chives and/or chopped parsley |

* a selection of fresh herbs tied in a bunch.

Put the lentils in the water with the *bouquet garni*. Leave to soak overnight if wished; this shortens the cooking time. When ready to cook add the yeast extract and chopped onions, then cover the pan. Simmer for about 1 hour, if the lentils have not been soaked, but only about 45 minutes if they were left in water overnight. Add the chopped carrots and chopped celery. Taste the soup, add a little sea salt and paprika or curry powder. Continue cooking for about 15-20 minutes. Either serve the soup like this, or put into the warmed liquidiser and switch on until a smooth soup. The herbs can be removed before liquidising or untied and emulsified with the lentils, etc. If preferred, sieve the soup. Top with chopped chives and/or parsley.

*Serves 6-7*

There are many ways of varying this soup, see below.

## To vary

*Add wheat germ and brewer's yeast* to turn this into a particularly 'flavoursome' and creamy textured soup. I added 2 tablespoons wheat germ and 1 tablespoon brewer's yeast to the lentil mixture when it was in the liquidiser, then reheated gently for a few minutes. You can, of course, increase the amounts if wished. Top with chopped nuts, if liked.

*Add 2-3 crushed cloves of garlic* for a very piquant flavour. Cook with lentils and onions.

*Split pea soup:* ✳✳ use split peas in place of lentils. Include plenty of mint with the other herbs.

# Green pea soup ✳✳

| Imperial | American |
|---|---|
| 1-1½ lb. fresh peas | 1-1½ lb. fresh peas |
| 2 pints water | 5⅓ cups water |
| 4-5 spring onions | 4-5 scallions |
| small piece celery or cucumber | small piece celery or cucumber |
| small piece lettuce | small piece lettuce |
| sea salt to taste | sea salt to taste |
| 1 teaspoon brown sugar | 1 teaspoon brown sugar |
| sprig mint* | sprig mint* |
| sprig parsley* | sprig parsley* |

| **to garnish** | **to garnish** |
|---|---|
| chopped parsley | chopped parsley |
| few peanuts or cashew nuts | few peanuts or cashew nuts |

* chopped if you have no liquidiser.

Wash and shell the peas. Heat about one-third of the water, drop in the pea pods. Cook until tender (about 15 minutes). Either remove the pea pods for a thin stock, or sieve or emulsify the pods with the liquid for a thicker stock. If you wish to make a purée soup, the onions, etc., need a little chopping, but for a vegetable broth, cut or shred the vegetables finely. Bring the rest of the water to the boil, add the peas, other vegetables, salt, sugar and herbs. Cook for 10-12 minutes, add the pea stock and heat. Either serve the soup like this, or rub through a sieve, or put into a warmed liquidiser and switch on until smooth. Serve this soup hot or cold, topped with the chopped parsley and the nuts.

*Serves 4-6*

# Green pea and asparagus soup ✳✳

| Imperial | American |
|---|---|
| 1½ pints water | 4 cups water |
| 8 oz. shelled peas | 2 cups shelled peas |
| small bunch spring onions | small bunch scallions |
| small bunch asparagus | small bunch asparagus |
| shake of paprika | shake of paprika |
| 1 tablespoon chopped mint | 1 tablespoon chopped mint |

Divide the water into two pans. Bring to the boil, put the peas and spring onions in one pan and the asparagus in the other. Cook until both vegetables are tender. Cut the tips from the asparagus for garnish, and put the vegetables and liquid into the liquidiser, switch on until smooth. Top with the paprika, mint and asparagus tips.

*Serves 4-6*

# SALADS

key to stars see page 5

Many of the salad recipes in the next pages are ideal for a 'complete meal', but also could be served as a pleasant hors d'oeuvre. This is why the portions are given for both purposes. Never allow your salads to be dull—incorporate fruits in season, nuts, herbs, etc., and try a dressing with a new taste (see page 22).

It is important that ALL food is eaten as soon as possible after purchase, but salads lose much of their appeal, and food value, if the ingredients are not *very* fresh.

If storing salad ingredients in a refrigerator keep them well covered in the special container, or wrap in polythene or foil. Store as far away from the freezing compartment as possible.

## Bases for green salads
Do not allow green salads to become monotonous. On the right is a recipe for a mixed green salad, but this can be changed by the choice of the basic vegetable, it could be:
*lettuce* of various kinds, mix one or more kinds in a salad, or choose *curly green endive*
*cabbage*—green, white and red and cabbage greens. If the vegetable is shredded, scalded for 1 minute in rapidly boiling water, drained then cooled, it develops more mineral salts
*young turnip* or *beet tops*, *sprouts*, *spinach*, *dandelion leaves* and smaller tender *nasturtium leaves* all add variety.

## Preparing the ingredients for salads
Shredding, grating and slicing ingredients for salads takes an appreciable time. There are many appliances available to do this quickly and successfully, some are described on page 4. An inexpensive shredder/grater and mincer is shown on page 19, together with the salad made with this.

## Green salads

Green salads are the best accompaniment to main dishes, as well as being refreshing salads by themselves. It is traditional that all the ingredients, as the name implies, are green—so tomatoes, beetroot, fruit, etc., are generally omitted from a classic green salad. The salad, *without dressing*, is definitely ✵✵✵.

The dressing chosen is generally a Vinaigrette dressing, although I enjoy the Yoghourt 1000-Island one too. Both recipes are on page 22.

## Green salad de-luxe ✵✵✵

| Imperial | American |
|---|---|
| 1 lettuce* | 1 lettuce* |
| ½ small endive | ½ small chicory |
| 1 head chicory | 1 head endive |
| 1 small green pepper | 1 small green pepper |
| ¼-½ medium cucumber | ¼-½ medium cucumber |
| bunch watercress | bunch watercress |
| few celery curls (see sketches on page 17) | few celery curls (see sketches on page 17) |
| dressing (see page 22) | dressing (see page 22) |

*the salad is much more interesting if you mix two or even three types of lettuce.

Wash the green salad ingredients and shake in a salad shaker, or pat gently in a tea towel. Often lettuce is bruised by undue pressure, so do this carefully. Shred the lettuce and endive if wished, or use whole leaves (whichever gives the most interesting looking salad in the container—this can be varied of course depending upon the occasion). The chicory head can be separated into leaves or cut into rings. The green pepper can be cut into thin rings, tiny dice or strips. If you save a few seeds from the inside and add these to the dressing you make a salad dressing with a piquant 'hot' taste. The cucumber can be cut into slices or matchsticks, or use a mixture of shapes. Put into the serving bowl or on the dish, top with the celery curls. Toss in dressing *just before* serving. *Serves up to 8*

To prepare watercress, cut or break the bottom of the stalks—wash sprigs well

## Simple vegetable salads

### Celery and leek salad ❊❊

| Imperial | American |
|---|---|
| small head celery | small head celery |
| 2-3 small leeks* | 2-3 small leeks* |
| 1 orange | 1 orange |
| 1 tablespoon chopped parsley | 1 tablespoon chopped parsley |

*these have a more delicate flavour than the larger ones.

Wash the celery and leeks well. Remove the celery leaves to use as a garnish. Chop the best outer stalks (any not perfect can be added to soups, etc.) and the very tiny heart stalks, but make some curls out of the medium sized stalks. Remember this takes some time, so do it early. Cut the leeks into wafer-thin rings. Mix the chopped celery and chopped leeks together. Grate a very little rind from the orange and blend with the juice and the parsley. Spoon over the salad. Garnish with the celery leaves and curls. This is an excellent hors d'oeuvre.

*Serves 4-6 as a starter*

### To vary
Use mayonnaise, blended with the orange juice, or by itself if preferred.

Serve the crisp celery and leeks on top of orange segments or orange rings.

Use chicory in place of celery.

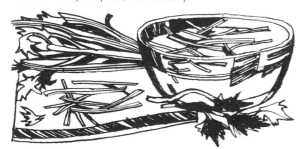

Put very thin long strips of celery into ice cold water

Leave for at least 1 hour, so they curl

### Cauliflower salad ❊❊❊

| Imperial | American |
|---|---|
| 1 small raw cauliflower | 1 small raw cauliflower |
| 4-6 tablespoons mayonnaise (see page 22) | up to ½ cup mayonnaise (see page 22) |
| 1-2 medium carrots | 1-2 medium carrots |
| 1-2 tablespoons black olives | 1-2 tablespoons black olives |
| watercress | watercress |

| **to garnish** | **to garnish** |
|---|---|
| red pepper (capsicum) or paprika and parsley | red pepper (capsicum) or paprika and parsley |

Wash the cauliflower and divide into small sprigs. Put the mayonnaise into a basin, add the grated carrots, chopped olives.

Arrange the cauliflower sprigs on a bed of watercress. Top with the mayonnaise and garnish with strips of red pepper, or paprika and coarsely chopped parsley.

This salad is an excellent hors d'oeuvre, or goes well with a nut roast, in which case use slightly less mayonnaise. *Serves up to 8 as an hors d'oeuvre or 4-6 with a main dish*

### Cucumber yoghourt salad (Riata) ❊❊❊

| Imperial | American |
|---|---|
| 1 medium cucumber | 1 medium cucumber |
| 1 clove of garlic (optional) | 1 clove of garlic (optional) |
| up to ½ pint yoghourt | up to 1⅓ cups yogurt |

| **to garnish** | **to garnish** |
|---|---|
| chopped chives | chopped chives |

The cucumber may be peeled if wished. Shred or dice this, and blend with the crushed clove of garlic and the yoghourt. Put into a dish and top with the chopped chives.

If wished, blend a little brown sugar or honey with the yoghourt.

This is an excellent accompaniment to a curry, or makes a very good hors d'oeuvre.

*Serves up to 8*

### To vary
Shredded leeks, or a mixture of leeks and celery, are excellent with, or instead of, the cucumber.

Add mixed herbs as a garnish instead of chives.

## Les crudites ✳✳✳

This is one of the best hors d'oeuvre to a meal, or will make a main meal with an egg, nuts or cheese.

Simply prepare individual dishes of salad—each dish containing one salad ingredient—then serve one or more dressings separately (see page 22). Choose:
*radishes*—they can be made into roses, see sketch

To make radish roses, cut as sketch, put into ice cold water

The radish rose opened out

*spring onions* (scallions) washed and left whole or again cut into a rose shape, see sketch

Cut down the stem of spring onions (scallions), put into ice cold water

The curled onion rose ready to use as a garnish, etc.

*grated swedes* or *turnips* and *grated beetroot*
*strips of celery* or celery curls (see page 17)
*carrots*—either tiny whole ones or strips
*a bowl of green salad* (either just lettuce, or a mixture of lettuce, endive or cabbage).

## Cucumber and orange salad ✳✳✳

| Imperial | American |
|---|---|
| 1 small cucumber | 1 small cucumber |
| 1 medium onion | 1 medium onion |
| 3 oranges | 3 oranges |
| 1 lettuce | 1 lettuce |
| little vinaigrette dressing (see page 22) | little vinaigrette dressing (see page 22) |
| **to garnish** | **to garnish** |
| little chopped fresh tarragon | little chopped fresh tarragon |

Put the unpeeled cucumber and the peeled quartered onion through the slicing attachment pictured opposite, or slice with a very sharp knife. Cut away the peel and pith from the oranges and cut into slices (this must be done by hand). Prepare the lettuce and put on to a flat dish, arrange the orange, cucumber and onion on this. Top with the dressing and tarragon. *Serves 6-8 as an hors d'oeuvre or 3-4 with a main dish*

**To vary**

*Beetroot and orange salad:* ✳ use sliced cooked beetroot in place of the cucumber. Put the salad together at the last minute, so the beetroot does not spoil the colour of the orange. Children will enjoy this salad.

*Fennel and orange salad:* ✳✳ use the base of a fennel in place of cucumber. This is an excellent salad with grilled fish. Fennel has an aniseed flavour.

## Mushroom and bean salad ✳

| Imperial | American |
|---|---|
| about 6 oz. raw small button mushrooms | about 2 cups raw small button mushrooms |
| few spring onions | few scallions |
| about 6 oz. cooked broad or haricot beans | about 1½ cups cooked broad or navy beans |
| little mayonnaise (see page 22) | little mayonnaise (see page 22) |
| **to garnish** | **to garnish** |
| chopped parsley | chopped parsley |

Slice the mushrooms and onions and mix with the beans and mayonnaise, top with parsley. *Serves up to 8 as an hors d'oeuvre or 3 with a main dish*

18

Cucumber and orange salad, page 18

## Apple cole slaw ✿✿

| Imperial | American |
|---|---|
| ½ small white cabbage | ½ small white cabbage |
| 3-4 oz. raisins | ½ cup seedless raisins |
| dressing of choice* | dressing of choice* |
| 1 teaspoon caraway seeds (optional) | 1 teaspoon caraway seeds (optional) |
| 4 oz. peanuts | ½ cup peanuts |
| 2-3 dessert apples | 2-3 dessert apples |
| little lemon juice or apple cider vinegar | little lemon juice or apple cider vinegar |

* mayonnaise turns this into a more nourishing meal—the amount is a personal choice.

Shred the cabbage finely. If wished you can scald this as the suggestion on page 16. Personally in a cole slaw I prefer it left raw. Put the raisins into the chosen dressing and leave to stand for a while. Blend the seeds and nuts with the dressing, then add the cabbage and half the chopped, sliced or grated apples. Pile into a dish and top with rings of apple, tossed in lemon juice, or vinegar, to keep them a good colour.
*Serves 4*

### To vary
A cole slaw is one of the classic salads and can be varied in so many ways. Serve with hot or cold dishes. Any dressing blends well with this cabbage salad. If you wish to make it very low in calories, use just lemon juice or apple cider vinegar. Below are other suggestions:

*Beetroot and raisin cole slaw:* ✿ blend shredded white or green cabbage with shredded beetroot (raw if possible) and raisins. Toss in mayonnaise or the egg and yoghourt dressing (see with the brown rice salad, page 21).

*Carrot cole slaw:* ✿✿✿ blend equal quantities of shredded red, white or green cabbage and shredded carrots. Add chopped parsley.

*Pepper cole slaw:* ✿✿ mix shredded white or green cabbage with shredded green and red peppers. Toss in vinaigrette dressing, made sweeter than usual with honey or brown sugar.

*Fruit cole slaw:* ✿ to ✿✿✿ mix chopped apples, oranges, pineapple, nuts, and dried fruit with shredded red or green cabbage; toss in dressing.

*Salads make a meal* if they include a protein food, as most salads on this and the next page.

## Potato cheese salad ✿

| Imperial | American |
|---|---|
| ¾-1 lb. cooked diced potatoes | about 2 cups cooked diced potatoes |
| 3-4 sticks celery, chopped | 1 cup chopped celery |
| olives | olives |
| 1 lettuce | 1 lettuce |

| **for the dressing** | **for the dressing** |
|---|---|
| ¼ pint yoghourt | ⅔ cup yogurt |
| 1-2 oz. Danish blue cheese | 2 tablespoons Danish blue cheese |

Blend the potatoes and celery and olives. Put on to a bed of crisp lettuce. Blend the yoghourt and cheese together, spoon over the potatoes.
*Serves 4*

### To vary
Potato salads can be varied in many ways. If possible mix while the potatoes are hot, then allow to cool. Obviously though, one can use left-over cooked potatoes in this salad. A basic potato salad is made by mixing the sliced or diced cooked potatoes, chopped or grated onion or spring onions (scallions) or chives, with a dressing (any of the dressings on page 22 are suitable, and the egg and yoghourt dressing on the right). Top with chopped parsley and/or chopped chives and/or chopped mint. Shredded cucumber, celeriac, red or green peppers also blend with potato salad.

## Cheese Waldorf salad ✿✿✿

| Imperial | American |
|---|---|
| 1 or 2 dessert apples | 1 or 2 dessert apples |
| 2-3 sticks celery, chopped | ¾ cup chopped celery |
| 2 oz. walnuts, chopped | ½ cup chopped walnuts |
| ¼ pint yoghourt | ⅔ cup yogurt |
| 1 lettuce or endive | 1 lettuce or chicory |
| 8 oz. cottage cheese | 1 cup cottage cheese |

| **to garnish** | **to garnish** |
|---|---|
| about ¼ medium melon | about ¼ medium melon |
| chopped basil and/or chervil | chopped basil and/or chervil |

Core, but do not peel the apples; chop and mix with the celery, walnuts and yoghourt. Pile on to a bed of lettuce or endive. Arrange the cottage cheese round the apple mixture, with a garnish of diced melon, or melon balls and chopped herbs.
*Serves 4*

## Lentil tomato salad ❀❀

| Imperial | American |
|---|---|
| 2 oz. lentils | ¼ cup lentils |
| 1 onion | 1 onion |
| ½ pint water | 1⅓ cups water |
| ½ teaspoon yeast extract | ½ teaspoon yeast flavoring extract |
| *bouquet garni* | *bouquet garni* |
| 4-6 large tomatoes | 4-6 large tomatoes |
| very little celery | very little celery |
| few olives | few olives |
| 2 oz. grated cheese | ½ cup grated cheese |
| little vinaigrette dressing (page 22) | little vinaigrette dressing (page 22) |
| lettuce | lettuce |

Put the lentils and chopped onion in the water with the yeast extract and soak overnight if possible, then add the herbs and simmer for about 1¼ hours. Check that the mixture does not become too dry and burn. If the lentils are not soaked, then allow about 1½ hours simmering. (In a pressure cooker they take only about 10 minutes at 15 lb. pressure, and you need just under the ½ pint (1⅓ cup) water.) Cut the tops off the tomatoes, scoop out the pulp and blend with the lentil mixture, the finely chopped celery, olives and cheese, and moisten with a little dressing. Pile back into the tomato cases and serve on a bed of lettuce.  *Serves 4-6*

## Apple and avocado salad ❀

| Imperial | American |
|---|---|
| about 6 tablespoons sweet-sour dressing (page 22) | about ½ cup sweet-sour dressing (page 22) |
| 1 small grapefruit | 1 small grapefruit |
| 1 large or 2 smaller ripe avocado pears | 1 large or 2 smaller ripe avocado pears |
| 2-3 dessert apples | 2-3 dessert apples |
| 1 lettuce or endive | 1 lettuce or chicory |
| 8 oz. cottage cheese | 1 cup cottage cheese |
| 3 oz. cashew nuts | ½ cup cashew nuts |

Put the dressing in a basin. Cut the peel and pith from the grapefruit over the basin, so any juice blends with the dressing. Divide the grapefruit into segments. Halve the avocado, remove the stone, skin and slice neatly, and put into the dressing. Core the apples, do not peel, then slice and moisten with dressing. Arrange the grapefruit, apple and avocado slices on the lettuce or endive. Pile the cheese in the centre and top with nuts. Spoon any extra dressing over the fruits. (See picture, page 23.)  *Serves 4-6*

Avocado pears are a most nutritious fruit.

## Brown rice salad ❀❀

| Imperial egg and yoghourt dressing | American egg and yogurt dressing |
|---|---|
| 1 egg | 1 egg |
| ¼ pint yoghourt | ⅔ cup yogurt |
| 3 tablespoons lemon juice or apple cider vinegar | 3-4 tablespoons lemon juice or apple cider vinegar |
| good pinch sea salt | good pinch sea salt |
| shake cayenne pepper | shake cayenne pepper |
| 1-2 teaspoons honey or brown sugar | 1-2 teaspoons honey or brown sugar |

| **for the salad** | **for the salad** |
|---|---|
| 4 oz. brown rice | ½ cup brown rice |
| 2-3 hard-boiled eggs (optional) | 2-3 hard-cooked eggs (optional) |
| 4-6 oz. cottage cheese | ½-¾ cup cottage cheese |
| 1 green pepper | 1 green pepper |
| 4 sticks celery, chopped | 1 cup chopped celery |

| **to garnish** | **to garnish** |
|---|---|
| 2 tablespoons chopped fresh herbs* | 2-3 tablespoons chopped fresh herbs* |
| sliced tomatoes | sliced tomatoes |
| sliced cucumber | sliced cucumber |
| watercress | watercress |
| lettuce | lettuce |

* parsley, chives, rosemary.

To make the dressing: put the egg, yoghourt, lemon juice or vinegar, salt, pepper and honey or sugar into a basin over hot water, or the top of a double saucepan, and stir over HOT, but not boiling, water until it thickens. Meanwhile cook the rice (as page 38). Blend the hot rice with the hot dressing, add the chopped eggs, cheese, diced pepper (remove the core and seeds), and the celery. Form into a pile on the serving dish, and top with the herbs. Garnish with rings of tomato and cucumber. This dish is equally good if the rice is served hot or cold. If serving cold, add sprigs of watercress and/or lettuce to the dish. If serving hot, make a separate salad of watercress and lettuce.  *Serves 4-6*

## Salad dressings

There are many natural ingredients that make excellent salad dressings. If you are anxious to lose weight, then use just lemon juice or apple cider vinegar as a simple dressing. Spoon over the salad.

If you prefer a sweeter flavour to your dressing, blend the juice or vinegar with brown sugar or honey and a little paprika.

## Flavour-full vinaigrette dressing ❋❋❋

| Imperial | American |
|---|---|
| 1 clove of garlic (optional) | 1 clove of garlic (optional) |
| good pinch sea salt | good pinch sea salt |
| shake of paprika | shake of paprika |
| shake of cayenne pepper | shake of cayenne pepper |
| 1-2 teaspoons honey (optional) | 1-2 teaspoons honey (optional) |
| 6 tablespoons olive oil | ½ cup olive oil |
| 3 tablespoons lemon juice* | ¼ cup lemon juice* |
| 1 tablespoon mixed chopped fresh herbs | 1¼ tablespoons mixed chopped fresh herbs |

* or use a mixture of lemon juice and cider vinegar, or mix orange, grapefruit and lemon juice (the proportion of juice can be higher if wished, but is generally 2 parts oil to 1 part lemon juice, or the alternative).

Skin the garlic and crush with a garlic press or the tip of a knife. If you put the salt on a board it helps to crush the garlic. Put the garlic, salt, paprika and cayenne pepper into a basin or on to a large plate with the honey. Gradually blend in the oil, then lemon juice and herbs (depending upon type of salad). *Serves up to 8*

## Yoghourt 1000-Island dressing ❋❋❋❋

| Imperial | American |
|---|---|
| 1 hard-boiled egg, chopped | 1 hard-cooked egg, chopped |
| 1 tablespoon chopped black olives | 1¼ tablespoons chopped black olives |
| ½-1 teaspoon chopped onion | ½-1 teaspoon chopped onion |
| 3-4 tablespoons finely chopped celery heart | ½ cup finely chopped celery heart |
| ¼ pint yoghourt | ⅔ cup yogurt |

Mix all the ingredients together. *Serves 4-5*

## Mayonnaise ❋

| Imperial | American |
|---|---|
| 2 egg yolks | 2 egg yolks |
| 1-2 teaspoons brown sugar or honey | 1-2 teaspoons brown sugar or honey |
| pinch sea salt | pinch sea salt |
| shake of paprika | shake of paprika |
| up to ½ pint corn or olive oil | up to 1⅓ cups corn or olive oil |
| up to 3 tablespoons lemon juice or apple cider vinegar | up to 3½ tablespoons lemon juice or apple cider vinegar |

Put the egg yolks into a basin with the sugar or honey, the salt and the paprika. Gradually 'drip' in the oil, stirring all the time. This can be added more quickly as the mayonnaise begins to thicken. Add the lemon juice or cider vinegar to taste.

If using an electric whisk: follow the method above.

If using a liquidiser: put the egg yolks, sugar or honey, salt and paprika into the goblet. Switch on for a few seconds only. Remove the cap from the lid, or use a foil 'lid', see page 4. With the motor running at a medium speed, add the oil steadily. When all the required amount of oil has been added, pour in the lemon juice or vinegar gradually.

A tablespoon of hot water added at the end of mixing gives a very creamy mayonnaise.
*Serves up to about 10 (depending upon the type of salad and personal taste)*

## Sweet-sour dressing ❋

| Imperial | American |
|---|---|
| 6 tablespoons mayonnaise | ½ cup mayonnaise |
| up to 2 tablespoons honey or brown sugar | up to 2¼ tablespoons honey or brown sugar |
| 4 tablespoons tomato juice | ⅓ cup tomato juice |
| 1-2 tablespoons lemon juice | 1-2 tablespoons lemon juice |

Blend all the ingredients together. Do this gradually, unless using the liquidiser.

If using the liquidiser you can substitute 2-3 tomatoes for the tomato juice.

Apple cider vinegar can be chosen in place of lemon juice, and a generous amount of chopped herbs (dill, chives, parsley, fennel) can be added. *Serves up to 6*

Apple and avocado salad, page 21,
Avocado honey ice, page 61

# VEGETABLE DISHES

key to stars see page 5

The recipes in this chapter use vegetables to provide main dishes. All too often the food value and flavour of a delicious vegetable is lost by over-cooking. When possible eat suitable vegetables uncooked, but always aim to cook for the shortest time possible, and to serve as quickly as possible after they are ready.

The wide range of vegetables available means you have a splendid selection throughout the year. Many people are surprised to learn just how vegetables can provide much of the protein, the carbohydrates, minerals and vitamins the body needs for perfect health. More details are given on pages 5 to 8.

## Preparing vegetables

Check the quality of the vegetables you buy. Of course it is ideal if you can grow many of them in your own garden, for they can be picked just before required, so are perfectly fresh, and you can determine the kind of soil, etc., in which they are grown. Often though, it is possible to find shops which specialise in local grown and organic vegetables. Try to buy sufficient for one or two days, for vegetables deteriorate in flavour and food value when stale.

Do not cut or shred vegetables too long before cooking. Preparation, washing, and cooking should follow each other as quickly as possible. The mineral salts and many of the vitamins are soluble in water, so prolonged soaking means these are lost before you begin cooking. Always save the water in which the vegetables have been cooked. It can be added to sauces, put into vegetable drinks, etc. Try to dish up the vegetables as soon as possible after cooking. You will notice that I add little seasoning, this is because vegetables, if cooked correctly, i.e. in the minimum of water, etc. (see the next column) retain much of their flavour. If you wish to add sea salt, do not be too lavish.

## Cooking vegetables

The way vegetables are cooked is all important. To boil vegetables, have the minimum of water. Bring this to the boil, add the vegetables gradually, rather than all at once, so the water does not cease boiling. Put the lid on the pan, cook for the shortest time possible. Green vegetables will keep a good colour, and should be sufficiently firm to retain their 'nutty' flavour and some crispness.

When the vegetables are cooked, strain, but keep the liquid, toss the vegetables in a little vegetarian fat or margarine, or add a small quantity of apple cider vinegar to green vegetables for additional flavour.

Root vegetables should be cooked in the same way, tossed in vegetarian fat or margarine and herbs, or baked in the oven until tender.

## Stuffed aubergines (egg plants) ✽✽✽

| Imperial | American |
|---|---|
| 4 medium aubergines | 4 medium egg plants |
| little sea salt | little sea salt |
| 2 onions | 2 onions |
| 2 oz. margarine | $\frac{1}{4}$ cup margarine |
| 2 oz. cooked rice | $\frac{1}{4}$ cup cooked rice |
| 2-3 large tomatoes | 2-3 large tomatoes |
| 4 oz. grated Cheddar cheese | 1 cup grated Cheddar cheese |
| shake cayenne pepper | shake cayenne pepper |

Wash the aubergines and dry. If you dislike the slightly bitter taste of aubergine skin, score the skin with a sharp knife, sprinkle lightly with salt, and allow to stand for 15 minutes. This makes a much milder flavour. Halve the aubergines lengthways and put into boiling water for 5 minutes only. Lift out and drain. Scoop out some of the centre pulp, chop this fairly finely. Peel the onions, chop finely and toss in most of the hot margarine for a few minutes, add the rice, chopped tomatoes, cheese, chopped aubergine pulp, and cayenne pepper. Spoon this mixture into the 8 aubergine 'shells'. Lift into a margarined dish, top with greased foil or greaseproof paper, and bake in the centre of a moderate oven, 350-375°F, Gas Mark 4-5, for 30-35 minutes.    *Serves 4*

## To vary

Use fairly large courgettes (zucchini) in place of aubergines; bake for about 25 minutes.

## Artichokes and mushrooms ❋❋❋

| Imperial | American |
|---|---|
| 4 globe artichokes | 4 globe artichokes |
| little sea salt (optional) | little sea salt (optional) |
| 1 onion | 1 onion |
| 1 tablespoon corn oil | 1 tablespoon corn oil |
| 4 oz. chopped mushrooms | 1 cup chopped mushrooms |
| 1 tablespoon chopped parsley | 1 tablespoon chopped parsley |

Trim the very outside leaves from artichokes. Cook in boiling water, adding a little salt if wished (or use 1 teaspoon yeast extract to flavour). Meanwhile, peel and chop the onion, cook in the corn oil, add mushrooms and parsley, heat thoroughly. Drain artichokes when tender (they take about 25 minutes), pull out the centre 'choke', this is the very heart of the vegetable. Fill with mushroom mixture and serve hot. *Serves 4*

### To vary
This also makes a good cold dish: blend a little salad dressing or apple cider vinegar with the mushrooms. Serve on a bed of lettuce.

## Stuffed beetroot—hot ❋❋❋

| Imperial | American |
|---|---|
| 8 small cooked beetroots | 8 small cooked beets |
| 2 oz. margarine | ¼ cup margarine |
| 4 oz. mushrooms, chopped | 1 cup chopped mushrooms |
| 2 teaspoons brewer's yeast | 2 teaspoons brewer's yeast |
| 2 teaspoons chopped parsley | 2 teaspoons chopped parsley |
| 2 oz. grated Cheddar cheese | ½ cup grated Cheddar cheese |

| for the topping | for the topping |
|---|---|
| 2 tablespoons grated cheese | 2-3 tablespoons grated cheese |
| 2 tablespoons soft wholemeal crumbs | 2-3 tablespoons soft wholewheat crumbs |

Scoop out the centre of the beetroots, leaving a good sized cavity in the centre. Chop the amount removed, then put into a basin. Heat the margarine and add the chopped mushrooms, fry until soft and tender. Add the yeast, parsley and grated cheese. Mix with the chopped beetroot. Pile into the centre of the beetroot 'cups'. Top with the cheese and crumbs, and put in a dish in a moderate oven for 20 minutes.
*Serves 4 as a main dish, 8 as an hors d'oeuvre*

## Stuffed beetroot—cold ❋❋

| Imperial | American |
|---|---|
| 8 small cooked beetroots | 8 small cooked beets |
| 1-2 oz. button mushrooms, chopped | about ½ cup chopped mushrooms |
| 4 oz. cottage cheese | ½ cup cottage cheese |
| 1-2 teaspoons chopped chives | 1-2 teaspoons chopped chives |
| 2-3 teaspoons chopped parsley | 2-3 teaspoons chopped parsley |
| 1 clove crushed garlic (optional) | 1 clove crushed garlic (optional) |
| about 12-16 black olives | about 12-16 black olives |
| lettuce or endive | lettuce or chicory |

Scoop the centre out of the beetroots. Dice the part removed and use this as a garnish.

Mix the chopped raw mushrooms, cottage cheese, chives, parsley, garlic and some of the chopped olives (save 8 for garnish).

Pile the cheese mixture into the cups, and top with black olives. Serve on a bed of lettuce or endive. *Serves 4*

### To vary
This is also a delicious hot dish: heat gently in a foil-covered dish until the cheese begins to soften, then serve at once.

## Carrots, Spanish style ❋❋

| Imperial | American |
|---|---|
| approximately 1 lb. young carrots | approximately 1 lb. young carrots |
| 2 tablespoons olive oil | 2¼ tablespoons olive oil |
| 1-2 cloves of garlic | 1-2 cloves of garlic |
| 1 onion | 1 onion |
| 3-4 large tomatoes | 3-4 large tomatoes |
| 1 red or green pepper | 1 red or green pepper |

Cook the carrots until tender, add a little sea salt or brown sugar to the boiling water for extra flavour if wished, but this is not really necessary.

Meanwhile, heat the oil, add the peeled chopped garlic, onion and tomatoes, simmer until nearly soft. Cut the flesh from the pepper into neat pieces, add to the rest of the ingredients, but heat for a few minutes only so the pepper retains its firmness. Add a few seeds from the pepper to give an interesting hot taste. Strain carrots, top with the vegetable mixture and serve hot or cold. *Serves 4-5*

Young turnips, swedes, parsnips, or cooked celery, can be served with a similar sauce.

## Beans and tomatoes ❀❀❀

| Imperial | American |
|---|---|
| about 1 lb. beans (French or sliced runner beans) | about 1 lb. beans (French or sliced green beans) |
| little sea salt | little sea salt |
| 1-2 teaspoons oil | 1-2 teaspoons oil |
| 1 lb. tomatoes | 1 lb. tomatoes |
| small bunch spring onions | small bunch scallions |

Put the beans into lightly salted boiling water and cook until tender. Strain, toss in the small amount of oil, then add the sliced tomatoes and chopped onions. Heat for about 5 minutes only, for the tomatoes and onions need to remain fairly firm. Serve by itself, or with an omelette or a nut roast. *Serves 4-6*

## French bean stew ❀❀❀

| Imperial | American |
|---|---|
| 1 lb. French beans | 1 lb. green beans |
| 2 small carrots | 2 small carrots |
| 1 small parsnip | 1 small parsnip |
| 2 medium potatoes | 2 medium potatoes |
| 1 lb. ripe tomatoes | 1 lb. ripe tomatoes |
| 2-3 onions | 2-3 onions |
| 1-2 cloves of garlic | 1-2 cloves of garlic |
| 2 tablespoons corn or other vegetable oil | 2¼ tablespoons corn or other vegetable oil |
| 1 green pepper | 1 green pepper |
| 1 tablespoon chopped parsley | 1 tablespoon chopped parsley |
| ½-1 teaspoon chopped chervil | ½-1 teaspoon chopped chervil |
| little sea salt | little sea salt |
| little yeast extract | little yeast flavoring extract |

Cut the ends off the beans. Wash and slice the carrots, parsnip, potatoes and tomatoes. Peel and chop the onions, and peel and crush the garlic cloves. Toss the onions and garlic in the hot oil, then add the tomatoes, and simmer until a fairly soft purée. Put in the other vegetables, except the green pepper, and cover the pan. Simmer gently for about 30 minutes, until the vegetables are soft. Dice the pepper, remove the core and nearly all the seeds. Add with a few seeds, if wished, to give a piquant flavour. Heat for 5 minutes, add the herbs and a little sea salt and/or yeast extract if wished.

*Serves 4-6*

*Note.* Both the recipes on this page can be made with fresh peas in place of beans. In winter use soaked, cooked dried peas, or dried beans.

## Celery with nuts ❀❀

| Imperial | American |
|---|---|
| 1 large or 2 smaller heads celery | 1 large or 2 smaller bunches celery |
| 1 tablespoon oil | 1 tablespoon oil |
| 2-3 oz. blanched almonds | ½ cup blanched almonds |

Remove the leaves, wash and quarter each head of celery. Heat the oil, brown the nuts. Top the cooked drained celery with the nuts and chopped celery leaves. Paprika and chopped herbs may be used with the leaves. *Serves 4*

## Stuffed cabbage rolls ❀❀

| Imperial | American |
|---|---|
| 8 young but fairly large cabbage leaves | 8 young but fairly large cabbage leaves |
| little sea salt | little sea salt |
| 1 lb. tomatoes | 1 lb. tomatoes |
| 3 oz. margarine | 6 tablespoons margarine |
| 2 medium onions | 2 medium onions |
| 2 oz. cooked brown rice | ¼ cup cooked brown rice |
| 1 tablespoon chopped parsley | 1 tablespoon chopped parsley |
| 2 oz. blanched almonds, chopped | ¼ cup blanched almonds, chopped |

Put the cabbage leaves into boiling salted water for about 4-5 minutes, until softened enough to roll. Lift out of the water, drain and put flat on a board. While the cabbage is softening, slice the tomatoes, put about a quarter of these into a basin and the rest into a casserole. Heat half the margarine in a pan and fry the peeled chopped onions for 5 minutes, until nearly soft. Add the onions to the tomatoes in the basin then stir in the rice, parsley and almonds. Divide between the softened cabbage leaves, roll firmly and tie with cotton. Put on to the tomato slices and top each cabbage roll with a little margarine. Cover the casserole with a lid or foil, and cook in the centre of a very moderate to moderate oven, 325-350°F, Gas Mark 3-4, for nearly 1 hour. *Serves 4*

**To vary**

Use wholemeal breadcrumbs in place of cooked rice.

Use 4 oz. (1 cup) grated Cheddar cheese in place of the almonds.

Boston baked beans, page 75

## Cooking cauliflower

Cauliflower is a most versatile vegetable. It is excellent cold in salads. Divide into sprigs and top with any of the salad dressings on page 22, and with grated cheese or chopped nuts.

*Cauliflower gratinée:* cook the cauliflower, strain, put in a heatproof dish, top with grated cheese and brown under the grill.

*Cauliflower mornay:* cook the cauliflower, save the liquid, use this to make a cheese sauce (see page 48). Coat the cauliflower with the sauce, top with chopped parsley and paprika.

## Stuffed cauliflower ❀❀

| Imperial | American |
|---|---|
| 1 medium cauliflower | 1 medium cauliflower |
| little sea salt | little sea salt |
| 2 oz. margarine | ¼ cup margarine |
| 1 medium onion | 1 medium onion |
| 2-3 large tomatoes | 2-3 large tomatoes |
| 2 oz. cooked sweet corn | ½ cup cooked kernel corn |
| 2 oz. peanuts | ⅓ cup peanuts |
| 2 oz. wholemeal breadcrumbs | ½ cup wholewheat breadcrumbs |
| 1 tablespoon wheat germ | 1 tablespoon wheat germ |

| for the topping | for the topping |
|---|---|
| 1 tablespoon chopped mixed fresh herbs | 1 tablespoon chopped mixed fresh herbs |

Boil the cauliflower in lightly salted water until just tender, but still sufficiently firm to be 'nutty'. While the cauliflower is cooking prepare the filling, so the cooked dish is eaten as soon as possible after cooking. To make the filling, heat the margarine, then add the chopped onion and tomatoes and simmer for about 5-6 minutes in the margarine until tender. Add the sweet corn, nuts, crumbs, wheat germ. When the cauliflower is cooked, scoop out the centre. If you support the very hot cauliflower in a steamer or colander you can handle it easily. Blend the chopped removed part with the filling. Pile back into the cauliflower shape. Top with chopped herbs and serve at once.   *Serves 4-5*

### To vary

1-2 chopped hard-boiled eggs may be added to the filling, or blend a little grated cheese with the mixture, just before filling, and top with grated cheese.

## Mushroom burgers ❀❀❀

| Imperial | American |
|---|---|
| 2 medium onions | 2 medium onions |
| 1-2 cloves of garlic (optional) | 1-2 cloves of garlic (optional) |
| 2 tablespoons corn or other vegetable oil | 2¼ tablespoons corn or other vegetable oil |
| 1 oz. wholemeal flour | 3 tablespoons wholewheat flour |
| ¼ pint water | ⅔ cup water |
| little yeast extract | little yeast flavoring extract |
| little sea salt | little sea salt |
| 8 oz. mushrooms, finely chopped | 2 cups finely chopped mushrooms |
| 3 oz. wholemeal breadcrumbs | 1 cup wholewheat breadcrumbs |
| 2 hard-boiled eggs, chopped | 2 hard-cooked eggs, chopped |

| to coat | to coat |
|---|---|
| 1 egg | 1 egg |
| about 1½ oz. fine wholemeal breadcrumbs | about ½ cup fine wholewheat breadcrumbs |

| to fry | to fry |
|---|---|
| 2-3 tablespoons oil | 2-3 tablespoons oil |

Chop the onions finely and crush the garlic cloves. Toss in the oil in a pan until just tender. Stir in the flour and cook for 2-3 minutes, then add the water, yeast extract and salt. Bring to the boil and cook until thickened. Add the mushrooms, crumbs and eggs and form into about 8 round cakes. Coat in beaten egg and crumbs, then fry until crisp and golden brown in hot oil.   *Serves 4*

### To vary

*Nut and mushroom burgers:* ❀ omit the hard-boiled eggs, add 3 oz. (½ cup) chopped pecan or walnuts. Coat with milk, or milk substitute, then the crumbs. Fry as above.

## Jacket potatoes ❈❈

| Imperial | American |
|---|---|
| medium potatoes | medium potatoes |
| margarine (see method) | margarine (see method) |

Wash and prick potatoes. Bake for about 1 hour in a moderately hot oven, 375-400°F, Gas Mark 5-6, or longer in a very moderate oven. When cooked, mark a cross on top with a sharp knife, cover with a tea cloth, leave for a few minutes. This has the effect of making a more 'floury' texture. Serve topped with vegetarian margarine or cottage cheese, or remove the pulp from the potato, mash with margarine or other vegetarian fat.

Alternatively mix with: grated cheese and a little yeast extract *or* fried mushrooms and chopped spring onions; make the pulp into a 'nest' in the potato case, add an egg, return to oven to set.

## Potato pancakes ❈

| Imperial | American |
|---|---|
| 4 medium potatoes (about 1 lb.) | 4 medium potatoes (about 1 lb.) |
| 2 eggs | 2 eggs |
| 1-2 tablespoons chopped parsley | 1-2 tablespoons chopped parsley |
| pinch sea salt | pinch sea salt |
| shake of paprika | shake of paprika |
| little milk or soya or plantmilk | little milk or soy or plantmilk |
| **to fry** | **to fry** |
| little corn or other vegetable oil | little corn or other vegetable oil |

Wash the potatoes, peel thinly if wished. Grate into a basin, add the eggs, parsley, salt, paprika, and enough milk to make a thick batter. Cover the basin and allow to stand for an hour before cooking. Beat again. Pour a little oil into the frying pan and heat. Spoon enough of the mixture into the pan to give a thin layer. Cook for 2-3 minutes, turn and brown on the second side. Keep hot on a plate, over hot water, while you cook the rest of the mixture. Serve hot with salads, or other vegetable dishes. *Serves 4*

### To vary
*Cheese and potato pancakes:* ❈ sandwich the pancakes together with cottage cheese, flavoured with chopped chives.

## Tomatoes plus

Tomatoes can be served in many ways: garnish cooked vegetables with sliced raw tomatoes; simmer tomatoes either by themselves, or with chopped garlic and onions to make a sauce; flavour with a little yeast extract, brown sugar or treacle (to give a very faint sweet flavour), add chopped fresh herbs, and pour over cooked vegetables, nut roasts, pulses or grain dishes.

*Stuffed tomatoes:* choose large tomatoes, cut a slice from the top and scoop out the pulp, chop and mix with grated or cottage cheese, chopped hard-boiled egg, sliced mushrooms, etc. Serve raw, or bake until tender.

## Tomato fondue ❈❈❈

| Imperial | American |
|---|---|
| 2 tablespoons corn or other vegetable oil | 2-3 tablespoons corn or other vegetable oil |
| 1 clove of garlic | 1 clove of garlic |
| 2 medium onions | 2 medium onions |
| 6 large tomatoes (about 1½ lb.) | 6 large tomatoes (about 1½ lb.) |
| 1 small apple | 1 small apple |
| ½-1 teaspoon chopped fresh marjoram or oregano | ½-1 teaspoon chopped fresh marjoram or oregano |
| ½-1 teaspoon brown sugar | ½-1 teaspoon brown sugar |
| pinch sea salt | pinch sea salt |
| shake of cayenne pepper | shake of cayenne pepper |
| **to garnish** | **to garnish** |
| carrots, celery, cauliflower | carrots, celery, cauliflower |

Heat the oil in a large pan or frying pan (the wider the pan, the quicker the mixture will thicken). Fry the crushed clove of garlic and peeled finely chopped or shredded onions until soft. Do not let them discolour. Add the skinned chopped tomatoes, the chopped apple, herbs, sugar, salt and pepper. Simmer for about 15 minutes until a thick mixture. Transfer to a shallow hot dish. Use as a party dip with small carrots, pieces of celery and sprigs of cauliflower arranged around the tomato mixture.

### To vary
*Cheese and tomato fondue:* ❈❈ add 8 oz. (2 cups) grated Cheddar cheese to the hot tomato mixture. Stir until the cheese has dissolved. Cut slices of wholemeal bread into cubes and use forks to dip into the hot mixture.

# VEGETABLE JUICES, ETC.

The juices of cooked vegetables should not be wasted, for they contain valuable mineral salts and vitamins. Several recipes suggest using the juices, or vegetable stock as it is called. They also make a pleasant drink. If you find them a little lacking in flavour, add yeast extract to taste. Serve vegetable stock hot, cold, or even iced, as a low-calorie alternative to soups, etc.

The recipes that follow, however, are for the juice of raw vegetables, and suggestions are given for blending and combining fruit and vegetable juices.

A juice separator enables you to extract the juice from even the hardest vegetables (carrots, potatoes, etc.), but as these are fairly costly I have also given suggestions for using a liquidiser (blender) as well.

As you need liquid with the vegetables in a liquidiser, the juices will be considerably less strong and will need additional flavouring in many cases. Most are ❅❅❅.

*Artichoke cocktail:* separate the juice from well washed globe or Jerusalem artichokes. Blend with a little apple or pineapple juice. If using a liquidiser, peel Jerusalem artichokes and put into the goblet with water to cover. Switch on until a purée, strain, then flavour the juice with apple or pineapple juice. The solid particles of artichoke can be added to soups or salads.

*Carrot cocktail:* as artichoke cocktail, but flavour with parsley juice (put this through the separator or into the liquidiser).

*Celery cocktail:* as artichoke cocktail, flavour with lemon juice, celery salt.

*Fennel cocktail* (particularly delicious): put both the root and leaves through the separator or into the liquidiser (covered with water plus a few slices of lemon). Add juice of fresh orange.

## More vegetable cocktails

All vegetables can be treated in the same way as suggested on the left; where a vegetable has a fairly bland taste, then give additional flavour with fruit juice. Where the vegetable is strongly flavoured, then it will need little if any additional flavour. Try the combinations suggested below:

*Cauliflower* blended with celery.
*Lettuce or endive* (chicory in U.S.A.) blended with pineapple or apple juice.
*Cabbage juice* blended with a very small amount of onion juice.
*Spinach juice* blended with a small amount of lemon and parsley juice.
*Tomato juice* mixed with celery salt, parsley and/or lemon juice. It is also very pleasant blended with orange juice. As tomatoes contain so much liquid there is no need to add water if using the liquidiser. Just put in the tomatoes, switch on, then strain. Add the parsley, slices of lemon or orange at the same time.
*Parsley and lemon cocktail:* put lemon juice into the liquidiser, add sprigs of parsley, switch on until the parsley has been finely emulsified.

## Vegetable mixtures

The recipes above and on the left produce liquid drinks, but the following mixtures are a thicker consistency and need to be served with a spoon. The fresh flavour of the vegetables is retained and enhanced by the other ingredients. Serve as a light snack or instead of a soup or hors d'oeuvre. These are all made in the liquidiser (blender) goblet; quantities are a matter of personal taste.

### Blend

*Artichokes* (globe or Jerusalem) with a little yoghourt, celery and apple.
*Beetroot* with yoghourt, lemon juice and parsley, or use portions of grapefruit in place of lemon juice, or banana and nuts, or apple and lemon.
*Carrots* with tomato or apple and nuts, or orange or green pepper plus a little yoghourt.
*Cauliflower or cabbage or lettuce* with celery, very little onion and parsley, or with apple.
*Spinach or kale or sprouts* with yoghourt, apple and lemon or orange.
*Tomato* with celery, apple and orange.

30

Ogen baskets, page 75

# DISHES USING PEAS, BEANS, LENTILS

These are grouped together as 'pulses', and that fairly dull-sounding name does not give any indication of the delicious dishes that can be made with these foods—and they also provide protein, among other essential nutrients.

The Indian cook has a wonderful range of dishes using Dhall (lentils) and I have given two of my favourites in this chapter.

Children generally love beans and should be encouraged to eat these in interesting ways.

## Bean casserole ✿✿✿

| Imperial | American |
|---|---|
| 8 oz. haricot beans | 1 cup navy beans |
| sea salt to taste | sea salt to taste |
| celery salt to taste | celery salt to taste |
| 4 large onions | 4 large onions |
| 6 large tomatoes | 6 large tomatoes |
| 1 tablespoon chopped parsley | 1 tablespoon chopped parsley |
| 1-2 teaspoons black treacle (optional) | 1-2 teaspoons molasses (optional) |
| little margarine | little margarine |

Cover the beans with cold water, soak overnight. Simmer steadily in the water in which they were soaked (or fresh water if preferred) until tender. This takes about 2½ hours in a covered pan, or 12-15 minutes only if using a pressure cooker at 15 lb. pressure. Add sea salt and/or celery salt to taste. Strain the beans from the liquid; keep 2-3 tablespoons for the casserole. The rest of the liquid can be used in soups. Chop 2 onions and 2 tomatoes very finely, mix with the beans, the bean liquid, parsley and treacle. Slice the rest of the onions very thinly, and the tomatoes more thickly. Put half the onions and tomatoes into a casserole, add the bean mixture, the rest of the onions and tomatoes and a little margarine. Cover the casserole and cook in the centre of a very moderate to moderate oven, 350-375°F, Gas Mark 4-5, for 40 minutes.
*Serves 3-4*

## Lentil loaf ✿✿✿

| Imperial | American |
|---|---|
| 8 oz. lentils | 1 cup lentils |
| 1¼ pints water | 3⅓ cups water |
| 1 teaspoon yeast extract | 1 teaspoon yeast flavoring extract |
| 2 oz. margarine | ¼ cup margarine |
| 1 clove of garlic | 1 clove of garlic |
| 2 onions | 2 onions |
| 2 tomatoes | 2 tomatoes |
| small piece of dessert apple | small piece of dessert apple |
| 3 oz. wholemeal breadcrumbs | 1 cup wholewheat breadcrumbs |
| 1 small green pepper | 1 small green pepper |
| ½ teaspoon chopped marjoram | ½ teaspoon chopped marjoram |
| ½ teaspoon chopped sage | ½ teaspoon chopped sage |
| 2 teaspoons chopped parsley | 2 teaspoons chopped parsley |
| little grated nutmeg | little grated nutmeg |
| 2 eggs | 2 eggs |
| little sea salt | little sea salt |
| little paprika | little paprika |

If the lentils are soaked overnight in the water they cook slightly more quickly. Simmer until tender and the liquid absorbed; this takes about 1 hour. Add the yeast extract while the lentils are hot. Meanwhile, heat most of the margarine in another pan, add the crushed clove of garlic, and peeled chopped onions, and fry until soft. Add to the lentils with the skinned chopped tomatoes, grated raw apple, breadcrumbs, diced green pepper, herbs, nutmeg, eggs, salt and pepper. Grease a loaf tin with the remainder of the margarine. Put the lentil mixture into the tin, and bake in the centre of a very moderate oven, 325-350°F, Gas Mark 3-4, for about 50 minutes, until firm. Serve hot with tomato sauce, page 43. *Serves 4-6*

### To vary
Use only 1½ oz. (½ cup) breadcrumbs and 2-3 oz. (½-¾ cup) finely chopped walnuts. Add a little finely chopped celery.

## Bean loaf ✿✿✿

Use the recipe above, but substitute cooked broad beans (fava or lima beans), or soaked and cooked haricot beans (navy beans), for lentils. The beans should be minced or chopped, so they blend with the rest of the ingredients.

## Lentil (Dhall) curry ✻✻

| Imperial | American |
|---|---|
| 8 oz. lentils | 1 cup lentils |
| 1½ pints water | 4 cups water |
| 2-3 teaspoons curry powder | 2-3 teaspoons curry powder |
| ¼ teaspoon sea salt | ¼ teaspoon sea salt |
| 2 oz. margarine or peanut butter | ¼ cup margarine or peanut butter |
| 3 onions | 3 onions |
| 3 tomatoes | 3 tomatoes |

Put the lentils into the boiling water with the curry powder and salt. Cook until tender and the thickness of a chowder (very thick soup). Meanwhile, heat the margarine or butter in another pan, cook the sliced onions and sliced tomatoes until soft. Stir into the lentil curry and serve with some of the side dishes mentioned on the right. *Serves 2-3 as a main dish, 4 as a light snack*

### To vary

Omit the curry powder, and use ¼-½ teaspoon chilli powder (very hot) or 1 thinly sliced red chilli pepper. Add also ½ teaspoon turmeric and 1 teaspoon cummin seed.

Add 1-2 tablespoons finely grated fresh or desiccated coconut.

*Lentil and cauliflower curry:* ✻✻ cook the lentil curry as the recipe above (it can be made a little hotter with additional curry powder, or by adding a pinch of chilli powder with the curry powder). Add a small quantity of coconut to the lentil curry. When the mixture is nearly ready, add small sprigs of raw cauliflower and turn in the curry mixture for a few minutes. This makes sure the cauliflower absorbs some of the flavour of the curry, but retains its firm texture.

*Haricot bean curry:* ✻✻ use soaked haricot beans (navy beans) in place of lentils. As they take longer to cook, increase the amount of liquid to 2 pints (5⅓ cups).

*Split pea curry:* ✻✻ use dried split peas in place of lentils, soak overnight, cook in 2 pints (5⅓ cups) liquid. Add chopped mint before serving.

*Fresh peas and beans in curry:* ✻✻ cook fresh peas and beans in the usual way, but use minimum of water. Cook the onions, etc., as recipe above, blend in the curry powder and peas or beans.

## Side dishes for curry

Serve some or all the following, to sprinkle over curry:

sliced cucumber blended with yoghourt ✻✻✻
sliced red and green peppers ✻✻✻
sliced tomatoes topped with chopped chives and parsley ✻✻✻
sliced onions or diced spring onions (scallions) ✻✻✻
nuts of various kinds ✻✻
freshly grated or desiccated coconut ✻✻
raisins or other dried fruit ✻
rings of orange ✻✻✻ and sliced bananas ✻

## Chapatis ✻✻

| Imperial | American |
|---|---|
| 8 oz. wholemeal flour | 2 cups wholewheat flour |
| water to mix | water to mix |

Mix the flour with enough water to give a firm rolling consistency. A good pinch of sea salt can be added, if wished.

Make the dough into about 12 small balls, then roll each ball out to a large round. If you have no griddle, then make rounds of a size to fit into a fairly solid frying pan. Cook in an ungreased frying pan for about 2 minutes on either side. Keep until ready to reheat.

To reheat these flat bread cakes, put into the ungreased pan for a minute, or grease the pan with a little vegetable oil and heat on either side. Serve as a side dish with curry.

*Makes about 12*

## Peas indienne ✻✻

| Imperial | American |
|---|---|
| 1 lb. shelled peas | 2 cups hulled peas |
| little water | little water |
| sea salt if wished | sea salt if wished |
| pinch brown sugar | pinch brown sugar |
| 1 oz. margarine | 2 tablespoons margarine |
| 3 oz. shelled peanuts | ¾ cup shelled peanuts |
| 1 teaspoon curry powder | 1 teaspoon curry powder |

Cook the peas in the lightly salted water, with a pinch sugar, until just tender.

Meanwhile, heat the margarine, toss the peanuts in this, add the curry powder and the strained peas. Mix together until the peas and nuts, etc., are well blended. Serve hot or cold.

*Serves 4*

# Curried lentil fritters ❊

| Imperial | American |
|---|---|
| 8 oz. lentils | 1 cup lentils |
| ¾ pint water | 2 cups water |
| 2-3 teaspoons curry powder | 2-3 teaspoons curry powder |
| ¼ teaspoon sea salt | ¼ teaspoon sea salt |
| 2 oz. margarine or peanut butter | ¼ cup margarine or peanut butter |
| 3 onions | 3 onions |
| 3 tomatoes | 3 tomatoes |
| 1 oz. wholemeal breadcrumbs | ⅓ cup wholewheat breadcrumbs |

| **to fry** | **to fry** |
|---|---|
| 2-3 tablespoons corn oil | 2-3 tablespoons corn oil |

Cook the lentils with the water, curry powder and salt until tender, and a dry mixture. This is considerably less water than usual, so be careful the mixture does not burn as it cooks. Meanwhile, heat the margarine or butter and fry the finely chopped onions and tomatoes until a smooth thick mixture. Add to the lentils with the crumbs. Heat the oil in a large pan and drop spoonfuls of the lentil mixture in this; fry for about 2 minutes on the under-side, turn and fry on the second side. Drain, and serve piping hot with green salad. *Serves 4*

# Green pea and corn fritters ❊

| Imperial | American |
|---|---|
| 8 oz. cooked peas | 1½ cups cooked peas |
| 4 oz. cooked sweet corn | ¾ cup cooked kernel corn |
| 1 egg | 1 egg |
| 4 oz. wholemeal flour | 1 cup wholewheat flour |
| pinch sea salt | pinch sea salt |
| 2-3 teaspoons chopped fresh herbs (chives, mint, etc.) | 2-3 teaspoons chopped fresh herbs (chives, mint, etc.) |
| 1 tablespoon wheat germ | 1 tablespoon wheat germ |
| about ¼ pint milk or water | about ⅔ cup milk or water |

| **to fry** | **to fry** |
|---|---|
| 3-4 tablespoons corn oil | 3-4 tablespoons corn oil |

Mix the peas, corn, egg, flour, salt, herbs and wheat germ. Gradually add enough milk or water to make a thick batter. Heat half the oil in a pan, drop spoonfuls of the mixture into this, fry steadily until golden brown on both sides, and cooked. Remove, drain on absorbent paper, keep hot while frying second batch. These are excellent with salad for a light meal. They can be sprinkled with cheese, if wished. *Serves 5-6*

# Swedish beans ❊❊

| Imperial | American |
|---|---|
| 8 oz. haricot beans | 1 cup navy beans |
| 1½ pints water | 4 cups water |
| sea salt to taste | sea salt to taste |
| 2 teaspoons chopped onions | 2 teaspoons chopped onions |
| 1 tablespoon apple cider vinegar | 1 tablespoon apple cider vinegar |
| 1 tablespoon black treacle | 1 tablespoon molasses |
| ½ tablespoon brown sugar | ½ tablespoon brown sugar |
| 1 oz. margarine | 2 tablespoons margarine |
| 1 oz. wholemeal flour | 3 tablespoons wholewheat flour |

| **topping** | **topping** |
|---|---|
| little yoghourt | little yogurt |
| chopped parsley | chopped parsley |

Soak the beans overnight in the cold water. Next day, simmer in the same, or fresh water, with the salt to taste, until tender. This takes about 2½ hours in a saucepan. If necessary lift the lid for the last ½ hour so the liquid is reduced to about ¾ pint (2 cups). If using a pressure cooker, allow only about 8 minutes at 15 lb. pressure, allow the pressure to drop, then lift the lid and allow the liquid to evaporate, as above. Stir in all the ingredients except the flour and topping, blend well. Mix the flour with a very little cold water and stir into the beans and liquid, then stir over a low heat until a smooth thickened sauce. Serve very hot, topped with the yoghourt and parsley. *Serves 3-4*

**To vary**

Split peas can be used instead of beans, but reduce the amount of treacle (molasses) to 1 teaspoon, and add a generous amount of chopped mint to the topping.

# Paprika beans ❊❊

This recipe is similar to Swedish beans above, but omit black treacle (molasses) and sugar. Add a few sticks chopped celery, 2 more chopped onions, and 2-3 chopped tomatoes to the beans towards the end of the cooking period. Stir in the vinegar and margarine as recipe above. Blend the 1 oz. (3 tablespoons) flour plus 2-3 teaspoons paprika with a little cold water. Add to the bean mixture, and stir until thickened. Top with yoghourt and parsley.

*Serves 4-6*

# Chilli with beans—country-style ✻✻

| Imperial | American |
|---|---|
| 8 oz. haricot beans | 1 cup navy beans |
| 1½ pints water | 4 cups water |
| sea salt to taste | sea salt to taste |
| 2 onions | 2 onions |
| 4 tomatoes | 4 tomatoes |
| 1 chilli pepper | 1 chili pepper |
| 1-2 teaspoons chilli powder | 1-2 teaspoons chili powder |
| 2 oz. margarine | ¼ cup margarine |
| 2-3 tablespoons chopped parsley | 2-3 tablespoons chopped parsley |

Soak and cook the beans as the Swedish beans on page 34, but allow the liquid to evaporate until barely ½ pint (1⅓ cups) is left. Meanwhile, chop the onions and tomatoes and cut the chilli pepper into tiny pieces. Blend with the powder. *Remember the chilli and the powder are very hot* so if you have never before made this, or any similar dish, use only the powder, and add this very sparingly. Toss the onions, etc., in the hot margarine, and when quite soft add to the beans and the liquid left in the pan. Stir over a low heat until blended. Top with the parsley, and serve very hot. *Serves 4-5*

# Vegetable stew ✻✻✻

If a vegetable stew contains a proportion of pulses it is a most satisfying dish.

| Imperial | American |
|---|---|
| 4 oz. haricot beans | ½ cup navy beans |
| 2 pints water | 5⅓ cups water |
| sea salt to taste | sea salt to taste |
| 2 oz. lentils | ¼ cup lentils |
| 2-3 onions | 2-3 onions |
| 3-4 carrots | 3-4 carrots |
| 1-2 turnips | 1-2 turnips |
| 1-2 courgettes | 1-2 zucchini |
| 3-4 tomatoes | 3-4 tomatoes |
| 1 green pepper | 1 green pepper |
| little chopped parsley | little chopped parsley |
| little chopped sage | little chopped sage |

Soak and simmer the beans in the water, as Swedish beans (page 34). At the end of 1½ hours add the lentils, and cook for a further ½ hour. Stir well, then add the prepared sliced vegetables in the order given, and complete the 2½ hours cooking. Add herbs just before serving. The vegetables may be varied according to the season. *Serves 4-6*

# Bean pop-overs ✻

| Imperial for the batter | American for the batter |
|---|---|
| 4 oz. wholemeal flour | 1 cup wholewheat flour |
| pinch sea salt (optional) | pinch sea salt (optional) |
| 2 eggs | 2 eggs |
| ¼ pint milk, soya or plantmilk | ⅔ cup milk, soy or plantmilk |
| 2 tablespoons water | 3 tablespoons water |
| little corn oil | little corn oil |

| for the filling | for the filling |
|---|---|
| 1 small onion | 1 small onion |
| 4 large tomatoes | 4 large tomatoes |
| little water | little water |
| about 8 oz. cooked haricot beans | about 1 cup cooked navy beans |

Make a batter with the flour, salt, eggs, milk and water. Brush about 12 patty tins with a little oil, and heat for a few minutes in a hot to very hot oven, 425-450°F, Gas Mark 7-8. Pour in the batter and bake for 15 minutes until well risen, then lower the heat for a few minutes to make sure the pop-overs are well cooked. Meanwhile, put the chopped onion and chopped tomatoes into a pan with a little water (use bean water if possible) and simmer until a sauce-like consistency. Add the beans and heat well. Lift the pop-overs out of the tins on to a hot dish, fill with the bean mixture and serve at once. *Serves about 6*

**To vary**

The filling above is a very bland one, suitable for children who do not like strong tastes, but it can be varied in many ways: use rather more onions, and toss in a little hot oil or margarine, then add chopped pepper, tomatoes, chilli powder or chopped chilli, then the beans, and season well with cayenne and celery salt.

*Celery and bean filling:* ✻ toss chopped celery with chopped onion in a little oil or margarine, then add chopped tomatoes, chopped herbs.

*Cheese and bean filling:* ✻ make a cheese sauce as the recipe on page 48, then add cooked haricot beans (navy beans), or cooked broad beans (fava or lima beans). Top with sliced uncooked tomatoes and serve at once.

*Curried lentil pop-overs:* ✻ make the curried lentils on page 33, spoon into the pop-overs. Serve with some of the side dishes on page 33.

# DISHES USING GRAINS

Many people have never tasted wheat germ and look quite horrified when it is suggested that this is an excellent breakfast dish, topped with fruit, etc. When they once eat it though, they are speedily 'converted', for it is not only good for you—it is a source of protein, vitamin B, etc.—it is also good to taste.

Other grains, such as oats, pearl barley, millet, polenta, etc., can also be used as the basis for interesting dishes.

## Muesli ✳✳

This is one of the finest dishes for breakfast, for it incorporates many valuable foods in an 'easy-to-eat' way. Encourage children to eat this before they go out. All too often parents 'cannot face' breakfast, and children copy adults and so go to school without having a good start to the day.

Muesli is easy to digest, as well as speedy to prepare. If you wish a change or feel that even this quick dish takes too long to get ready, your Health Food Store will be able to offer you a selection of similar foods in packet form. Try it for supper too.

| Imperial | American |
|---|---|
| 2 tablespoons rolled oats | nearly 3 tablespoons rolled oats (flaked) |
| 1-2 tablespoons finely chopped or ground nuts | 1-2 tablespoons finely chopped or ground nuts |
| 2 dessert apples | 2 dessert apples |
| 1-2 tablespoons raisins | 1-2 tablespoons raisins |
| 1 tablespoon honey | 1 tablespoon honey |
| 1-2 tablespoons lemon or orange juice | 1-2 tablespoons lemon or orange juice |
| little milk or yoghourt | little milk or yogurt |

Put the rolled oats into a basin, add the nuts, unpeeled grated apples, raisins, honey and fruit juice. Mix well, add sufficient milk or yoghourt to moisten. If the oatmeal is soaked overnight in cold water to cover you have a softer texture to the Muesli. *Serves 3-4*

## Variations on muesli

Instead of rolled oats use whole oats, or cracked wheat or barley. Soak overnight in cold water, then continue as the recipe on the left.

For additional flavour and nourishment, blend 1 tablespoon wheat germ with the other ingredients in muesli (recipe on the left).

Many people, children in particular, enjoy this dish blended with a little condensed milk. If using this sweetened milk you can omit the honey, or use rather sharp apples.

Omit the apples and use other fruit in season, i.e. bananas (increase the amount of lemon juice slightly, as bananas have less flavour), fresh apricots, peaches, etc.

If serving muesli as a dessert—top with extra fruit and nuts.

## Whole grain roasts, etc.

Whole grains have a good flavour as well as being highly nutritious. A grain roast can be served instead of meat, with tomato or brown sauce (page 43) and plenty of freshly cooked vegetables.

The grains may be varied, so the roast does not become monotonous. Use pearl barley, oats, whole wheat grains, buckwheat or millet (obtainable from Health Food Stores). If you soak the grains overnight the texture is softer, and some natural food experts prefer soaking for up to 3 days, changing the water often. Sufficient grain for several dishes may be soaked and cooked at one time. It will keep for several days in a cool place.

The weight of grains given is before soaking.

# Wheat roast ❀❀

| Imperial | American |
|---|---|
| 8 oz. whole grain wheat | 1 cup whole grain wheat |
| 1 pint water * | 2⅔ cups water * |
| 3 oz. margarine | 6 tablespoons margarine |
| 2 large onions | 2 large onions |
| 1 clove of garlic | 1 clove of garlic |
| 2 large tomatoes | 2 large tomatoes |
| 2 eggs | 2 eggs |
| ½ teaspoon chopped sage | ½ teaspoon chopped sage |
| 2-3 sticks celery | 2-3 sticks celery |
| 1 green pepper | 1 green pepper |
| sea salt to taste | sea salt to taste |

*if wheat has been soaked, use ¾ pint (2 cups) water.

Simmer the whole wheat grains in the water until tender; this takes about 1½-2 hours. The lid of the pan can be lifted towards end of cooking time, so that the water evaporates and leaves a fairly firm texture. Heat 1 oz. (2 tablespoons) of the margarine in a pan, toss the chopped onions and garlic and tomatoes in this until a thick purée. Add to whole wheat with the beaten eggs, sage, finely chopped raw celery, and finely chopped green pepper. Blend well and add salt to taste. Use half remaining margarine to grease a 2 lb. loaf tin, put in the mixture and cover with melted margarine. Bake for nearly 1 hour in the centre of a moderate oven, 375°F, Gas Mark 4-5, until crisp and brown. Turn out carefully and cut into slices.

*Serves 4-6*

### To vary

*Nut wheat roast:* ❀❀ add 4 oz. (½ cup) coarsely chopped cashew or other nuts.

*Sour sweet loaf:* ❀❀ add 2 teaspoons brown sugar, 2 oz. (about ⅓ cup) sultanas and the grated rind and juice of 1 lemon. Since this makes a softer consistency, add about 1 oz. (⅓ cup) soft wholemeal (wholewheat) bread-crumbs to the grain. Serve with apple sauce (see page 43).

Choose other grains suggested on page 36.

Add more seasoning, i.e. sea salt, celery salt, cayenne pepper, to the mixture.

*Rolled oat roast:* ❀❀ since rolled oats cook very quickly, i.e. about 10 minutes only, use only half the amount of water. Stir well to keep the mixture from becoming lumpy, proceed as the recipe above, season well.

# Whole grain and nut savoury ❀❀

| Imperial | American |
|---|---|
| 8 oz. whole grain (wheat, pearl barley, millet, etc.) | 1 cup whole grain (wheat, barley, millet, etc.) |
| ¾ pint water | 2 cups water |
| ¼ pint milk, soya or plantmilk | ⅔ cup milk, soy or plantmilk |
| 2 tablespoons corn oil | 3 tablespoons corn oil |
| 2 onions | 2 onions |
| 2 tomatoes | 2 tomatoes |
| 4 oz. button mushrooms | 1 cup button mushrooms |
| 2-3 oz. cashew nuts or blanched almonds | ½ cup cashew nuts or blanched almonds |
| 1 teaspoons yeast extract | 1 teaspoon yeast flavoring extract |
| 1 teaspoon chopped parsley | 1 teaspoon chopped parsley |
| sea salt to taste | sea salt to taste |

Soak the grain overnight, drain this. Simmer in the water and milk for 1 hour. If using the top of a double saucepan over boiling water, allow a little longer. The grains should not be completely cooked. Prepare the rest of the mixture. Heat the oil and fry the chopped onions, tomatoes and mushrooms until just tender. Put at the bottom of an ovenproof dish. Stir the cashew nuts or almonds, yeast extract and parsley into the cooked grains, then add sea salt to taste. (It is important to add the salt at the end, so you do not 'over-salt'.) Spoon over the savoury mixture, and bake in the centre of a very moderate to moderate oven, 350-375°F, Gas Mark 4-5, for 30 minutes. Serve hot with green salad.

*Serves 4-6*

# Whole grain soufflé ❀❀

| Imperial | American |
|---|---|
| 4 oz. whole grain (wheat, millet, etc.) | ½ cup whole grain (wheat, millet, etc.) |
| ½ pint water | 1¼ cups water |
| 1 teaspoon chopped parsley | 1 teaspoon chopped parsley |
| 4 eggs | 4 eggs |
| 2 oz. grated Cheddar cheese | ½ cup grated Cheddar cheese |
| sea salt to taste | sea salt to taste |
| cayenne pepper | cayenne pepper |

Soak and cook the grain until tender, add the parsley, egg yolks, cheese, salt and pepper, then the stiffly beaten egg whites. Cook in a greased soufflé dish in the centre of a moderate to moderately hot oven, 375-400°F, Gas Mark 5-6, for 35 minutes. Serve with tomato sauce, page 43.

*Serves 4-5*

# RICE DISHES

key to stars see page 5

The peoples of a vast part of the world base their diet almost entirely on rice. To our sophisticated palates, which have become accustomed to an unbelievable selection of foods, it may sound an impossible way to live. Of course we have no need to do this, but most of us would agree that rice dishes are generally practical and very pleasant. If you have never tasted the *brown unpolished rice*, you have no conception of just how much flavour rice itself has. It is brown rice that will ensure you have the maximum food value from each recipe.

## Flavouring rice

Brown rice has much natural flavour, but add a little brewer's yeast and wheat germ or yeast extract to the recipes, even when not specified in the recipe.

One or two teaspoons black treacle (molasses) may sound unusual in a savoury recipe but it is very pleasant, particularly where nuts and dried fruits are used.

Any cooked rice left over may be added to salads, soups and stuffings.

## Soaking rice

If the rice is soaked overnight, or even longer, it brings out the biochemic salts in the food. Put the rice into a basin and pour enough water over the rice to cover.

The recipes refer to the weight of rice *before* soaking, as naturally this is much heavier after absorbing the water. The rice will be softer after soaking, so use less liquid in the recipes, i.e. cut down by about one-third, so where a recipe states 'use 1 pint (2⅔ cups) liquid' you should use only ⅔ pint (1⅓ - 2 cups) with soaked rice. You will also need a little less cooking time to soften the rice.

## Curried rice ❊❊

| Imperial | American |
|---|---|
| 2 tablespoons corn oil | nearly 3 tablespoons corn oil |
| 2 onions | 2 onions |
| 1 dessert apple | 1 dessert apple |
| ½-1 tablespoon curry powder* | ½-1 tablespoon curry powder* |
| 1 pint water | 2⅔ cups water |
| 8 oz. brown rice | 1 cup brown rice |
| 2 teaspoons black treacle | 2 teaspoons molasses |
| sea salt to taste | sea salt to taste |
| 2-3 tablespoons grated coconut† | 2-3 tablespoons grated/shredded coconut† |
| little coconut milk | little coconut milk |
| 2-3 oz. sultanas | nearly ½ cup seedless white raisins |

* this is a generous amount, so use rather less if you do not like strongly flavoured dishes.
† or use 1-2 tablespoons desiccated coconut.

Heat the oil in a large pan, add the peeled sliced onions and apple, and heat for a few minutes. Blend in the curry powder and the water. Bring the water to the boil, then add the rice and treacle, stir well and cook for about 10 minutes. Taste, then add a little salt, if wished, and the rest of the ingredients. Continue cooking until the rice is tender and the liquid absorbed. Serve the curry with side dishes, see page 33.

*Serves 4*

## Spanish rice ❊❊

| Imperial | American |
|---|---|
| 8 oz. brown rice | 1 cup brown rice |
| 1 pint water | 2⅔ cups water |
| sea salt to taste | sea salt to taste |
| 2 onions | 2 onions |
| 1 clove of garlic | 1 clove of garlic |
| 3 tomatoes | 3 tomatoes |
| 4 oz. mushrooms | 1 cup mushrooms |
| 2-3 tablespoons olive oil | 2-3 tablespoons olive oil |
| pinch cayenne pepper | pinch cayenne pepper |

Put the rice with the water and salt into a pan. Bring the water to the boil, stir the rice well, put a lid on the pan, lower the heat and simmer for about 15 minutes, until the water evaporates and the rice is tender. Meanwhile, chop the vegetables and cook steadily in the hot oil. Add the rice and pepper, toss together and serve at once. This may be varied in many ways—add chopped pepper, peas or beans, or freshly chopped herbs.

*Serves 4-6*

## Tomato risotto ✳✳

| Imperial | American |
|---|---|
| 2 tablespoons corn oil | nearly 3 tablespoons corn oil |
| 1 onion | 1 onion |
| 1-2 cloves of garlic | 1-2 cloves of garlic |
| 8 oz. brown rice | 1 cup brown rice |
| ½ pint water | 1⅓ cups water |
| 1½ lb. tomatoes | 1½ lb. tomatoes |
| paprika | paprika |
| sea salt to taste | sea salt to taste |
| 1 tablespoon chopped parsley | 1 tablespoon chopped parsley |

| topping | topping |
|---|---|
| grated or cottage cheese | grated or cottage cheese |

Heat the oil in a *large* saucepan. Peel and chop the onion and garlic. Toss in the oil for a few minutes, then add the rice and turn in the onion and oil mixture until all the grains look shiny. Add the water and finely chopped tomatoes. Cook in an uncovered saucepan until the rice is tender and the liquid absorbed. This should be a soft, but not liquid mixture. Taste, add paprika and salt as required. Pile on to a hot dish and sprinkle with the parsley.

Top with grated cheese, or top each portion with cottage cheese. *Serves 4-6*

### To vary
Add a few sliced mushrooms and 1-2 finely diced or grated carrots to the mixture. I like to add the carrots towards the end of the cooking period so they retain their crisp texture, but this is purely a matter of personal taste.

## Mixed vegetable risotto ✳✳

Use the same recipe as tomato risotto but only about one-third the amount of tomatoes. Bring the water and tomatoes to the boil, add diced raw carrot, turnip, swede and a few uncooked peas. Continue as tomato risotto.

## Rice cutlets ✳✳

| Imperial | American |
|---|---|
| 3 oz. brown rice | scant ¼ cup brown rice |
| ½ pint water | 1⅓ cups water |
| 1 teaspoon yeast extract | 1 teaspoon yeast flavoring extract |
| 1 onion | 1 onion |
| 2 tomatoes | 2 tomatoes |
| 2 oz. margarine | ¼ cup margarine |
| 1 oz. wholemeal flour | ¼ cup wholewheat flour |
| ¼ pint milk or soya or plantmilk | ⅔ cup milk or soy or plantmilk |

| to coat | to coat |
|---|---|
| 1 egg or a little milk | 1 egg or a little milk |
| 2 oz. dried wholemeal crumbs | 1 cup dried wholewheat crumbs |

| to fry | to fry |
|---|---|
| little corn oil | little corn oil |

Put the rice into the cold water. Bring to the boil. Add the yeast extract and cook until all the liquid is absorbed and the rice is tender. Meanwhile, peel and chop the onion and tomatoes, and fry in the hot margarine until tender. Stir in the flour and cook for 2-3 minutes, then add the milk. Bring to the boil and cook until thickened. If using cow's milk, stir well to prevent the tomatoes curdling the milk. This does not happen with soya or plantmilk. Add the rice, and allow the mixture to cool. Form into 8 cutlet shapes, brush with beaten egg or milk, coat in the crisp crumbs. Fry in the hot corn oil. Serve hot with tomato sauce (see page 43). *Serves 4*

### To vary
*Cheese and rice cutlets:* ✳✳ add 2-4 oz. (½-1 cup) grated cheese, or 4 oz. (½ cup) cottage cheese, to the mixture. The cheese should be added to the cool rice and tomato mixture so that it does not become greasy.

*Egg and rice cutlets:* ✳✳ add 2 or 3 chopped hard-boiled eggs to the rice and tomato mixture.

*Rice and mushroom cutlets:* ✳✳ add 2-4 oz. (½-1 cup) chopped button mushrooms to the onion and margarine. Omit the tomatoes if wished.

*Rice loaf:* ✳✳ add an egg or 2-3 tablespoons more milk to the cutlet mixture. Put into a well greased tin, cover with greased foil and stand in a container of water. Bake for 45 minutes in the centre of a moderate oven.

# DISHES WITH NUTS

key to stars see page 5

How do you regard nuts—as a cake decoration or a pleasant 'nibble' at a cocktail party? If so you are neglecting one of the most interesting protein foods, which also contain fat (in the form of natural oil).

Nut dishes have both an interesting texture and a very definite flavour, and should never become monotonous, for there is such a variety of nuts from which to choose. Use different kinds of nuts in the recipes in this section; I have indicated which is the nut I prefer in each recipe, but I also make the dishes with other kinds. Often I mix several nuts together.

Health Food Stores have nut meats, which can be used in many well known dishes in place of meat. If you find coarsely chopped nuts indigestible, then grind them in the liquidiser (blender) or through a mincer, and serve nut dishes at mid-day, rather than later in the evening.

If nuts seem expensive to buy, remember they are taking the place of even more costly meat.

## Nut pilaff ❀❀

| Imperial | American |
|---|---|
| 1 tablespoon corn oil | 1 tablespoon corn oil |
| 8 oz. brown rice | 1 cup brown rice |
| 1 pint water | 2⅔ cups water |
| 1-2 teaspoons yeast extract (according to personal taste) | 1-2 teaspoons yeast flavoring extract (according to personal taste) |
| 4 oz. seedless raisins or sultanas | ⅔ cup raisins or seedless white raisins |
| 4-6 oz. pine or cashew or peanuts | ¾-1 cup pine or cashew or peanuts |

Heat the oil in a large pan and toss the rice in this. Add the water, bring to the boil, then stir in the yeast extract. Allow the mixture to cook until the rice is almost tender and the liquid nearly absorbed, then add the fruit and nuts, and heat for a few more minutes.    *Serves 4-6*

## Versatile nuts ❀❀

Nuts can be added to fruit breads, to small or large cakes, or used to make delicious petits fours or savoury 'bites'. They blend with: honey, mashed bananas, peanut butter in sweet sandwiches; or with cottage or cream cheese in savoury sandwiches. Sprinkle chopped nuts on top of soups or over salads. Encourage children to eat nuts or nutty 'sweetmeats', as page 41, instead of ordinary sweetmeats.

## Almond rice roast ❀

| Imperial | American |
|---|---|
| 1 lb. brown rice | 2 cups brown rice |
| 1½ pints water or vegetable stock | 4 cups water or vegetable stock |
| 1-2 teaspoons yeast extract | 1-2 teaspoons yeast flavoring extract |
| 4 oz. ground almonds | 1 cup ground almonds |
| 1-2 onions | 1-2 onions |
| 3 teaspoons chopped parsley | 3 teaspoons chopped parsley |
| 1 teaspoon chopped marjoram | 1 teaspoon chopped marjoram |
| 2 eggs | 2 eggs |
| 2 oz. margarine | ¼ cup margarine |

| **topping** | **topping** |
|---|---|
| 2-3 tablespoons blanched almonds (optional) | 3-4 tablespoons blanched almonds (optional) |

Cook the rice in the water as described under rice stuffing, page 45, add the yeast extract to the hot rice. Cool and fork to separate the grains, then mix with the ground almonds, grated onions, herbs and eggs. Grease a tin or dish with half the margarine, put in the rice mixture; top with the rest of the margarine. Bake in a moderately hot oven, 400°F, Gas Mark 5-6, for 30 minutes. Remove from the oven, put the almonds on top, and return to the oven for a further 5-10 minutes. Serve with tomato or apple sauce.    *Serves 6-8*

### To vary

*Rice and cheese roast:* ❀ omit the ground almonds, add 4-6 oz. (1-1½ cups) grated Chedder cheese. Top with peanuts in place of blanched almonds.

*Rice and nut meat roast:* ❀ use 4 oz. (½ cup) diced nut meat in place of ground almonds.

## Peanut bake ✻✻

| Imperial | American |
|---|---|
| 8 oz. shelled peanuts | 1 cup shelled peanuts |
| 3 oz. margarine or peanut butter | 6 tablespoons margarine or peanut butter |
| 3 oz. soft wholemeal breadcrumbs | 1 cup soft wholewheat breadcrumbs |
| 2 onions | 2 onions |
| $\frac{1}{4}$ teaspoon chopped sage | $\frac{1}{4}$ teaspoon chopped sage |
| $\frac{1}{2}$ teaspoon chopped thyme | $\frac{1}{2}$ teaspoon chopped thyme |
| sea salt (optional) | sea salt (optional) |
| cayenne pepper (optional) | cayenne pepper (optional) |

The peanuts may be minced, or put into the liquidiser goblet to give a smooth texture. While I find this gives a better result in the cutlets below, I prefer the nuts left whole in this particular recipe. Spread one-third of the margarine or peanut butter on the bottom of a shallow ovenproof dish, top with half the crumbs. Heat half the rest of the margarine or peanut butter, and fry the finely chopped onions until just soft. Mix with the peanuts, sage, thyme and seasoning. Spread over the crumbs, then top with the remaining crumbs and margarine or peanut butter. Bake in the centre of a moderate to moderately hot oven, 375-400°F, Gas Mark 5-6, until the topping is crisp and golden brown, approximately 25-30 minutes. Serve hot, with a mixed or green salad.

*Serves 4-5*

### To vary

*Brazil nut bake, etc.:* ✻✻ a more expensive version of this dish can be made with Brazil nuts (or other nuts). I chop Brazils very coarsely but leave hazelnuts, cashew nuts and walnuts in large pieces. When walnuts are fresh and very moist they are particularly good in the above recipe. If you dislike the bitter taste you must remove the skins, and I like a generous amount of salt with these particular nuts. Fresh cobnuts are also excellent in the bake.

*Peanut cutlets:* ✻ follow the instructions for the bake above, but use 2 oz. ($\frac{2}{3}$ cup) only of the crumbs and 1 oz. (2 tablespoons) of margarine or peanut butter, i.e. for cooking the onions. Mix all the ingredients together, bind with 1 egg. Form into cutlets, coat with egg and fine crumbs, then fry in hot oil or peanut butter. Serve hot or cold. These are excellent for a packed meal. If, as suggested in the bake, you mince or liquidise the nuts, you have a smooth texture; if you leave the nuts whole the cutlets are more difficult to shape and fry.

## Nut butters ✻✻

In many recipes I mention 'margarine'; you can of course obtain vegetarian margarine, which is made with vegetable and nut oils.

Often I suggest using peanut butter in a recipe, this is because I have found it gives an added flavour and interest to that particular dish. Peanut butter is extremely versatile, it can be used in baking, it is delicious on toast or bread, it blends with sweet or savoury ingredients, and children generally love its taste. It is, of course, very good for them.

You may be able to obtain other nut spreads or butters at your Health Food Stores and can use these on bread, biscuits, or as special 'toppings'. If they are not available then just make your own. Blend ground or finely chopped nuts of all kinds with creamed margarine. If the mixture is a little stiff for spreading, add a small amount of milk or fruit juice.

## Marzipan bars ✻

| Imperial | American |
|---|---|
| 4 oz. ground almonds | 1 cup ground almonds |
| 4 oz. brown sugar | just over $\frac{1}{2}$ cup brown sugar |
| 1 egg yolk | 1 egg yolk |

Blend the ingredients together, if necessary add a little egg white to bind the mixture, or a few drops lemon juice or sherry. Form into bar shapes and allow to harden.

### To vary

Add the grated rind of 1-2 oranges plus a very little orange juice.

Blend a little dried fruit and some chopped almonds, or other nuts, with the marzipan.

*Stuffed dates:* use some of the marzipan to stuff stoned dates (or stoned prunes).

If you do not wish to use an egg yolk, then bind the ground almonds with fruit juice. Other ground nuts make an equally good sweetmeat or coating for cakes, etc.

*Fruit and marzipan sandwich:* roll out the marzipan thinly, sandwich chopped dates, raisins, etc., with the marzipan; cut in squares.

## Nut balls ❄

| Imperial | American |
|---|---|
| 4 oz. stoned dates | nearly 1 cup stoned dates |
| 4 oz. dried figs | about $\frac{3}{4}$ cup dried figs |
| 4 oz. seedless raisins | about $\frac{3}{4}$ cup seedless raisins |
| 2 oz. desiccated coconut or grated coconut | $\frac{3}{4}$ cup flaked or shredded coconut |
| 2-4 oz. ground or finely chopped nuts | $\frac{1}{2}$-1 cup ground or finely chopped nuts |
| 1-2 teaspoons black treacle | 1-2 teaspoons molasses |
| **to coat** | **to coat** |
| desiccated coconut | flaked coconut |

Put the dates, figs and raisins through a mincer, or chop very finely. Mix with the coconut and nuts, and just enough black treacle to bind (do not make too soft). Form into tiny balls, roll in the desiccated coconut. These 'sweetmeats' are excellent for children, although, of course, they must clean their teeth after eating natural sweet foods such as these, as well as any other sweet things. *Makes about 24*

## Nut and raisin stuffing ❄❄

| Imperial | American |
|---|---|
| small head celery | small bunch celery |
| 1 onion | 1 onion |
| 4 oz. raisins | $\frac{3}{4}$ cup seedless raisins |
| 1 lemon | 1 lemon |
| 3 oz. soft wholemeal breadcrumbs | 1 cup soft wholewheat breadcrumbs |
| 2 oz. margarine | $\frac{1}{4}$ cup margarine |
| 6 oz. finely chopped nuts | $1\frac{1}{2}$ cups finely chopped nuts |

This stuffing is excellent with vegetables, meat or poultry. Remove the very outside stalks from the celery and chop this very finely, chop a few leaves as well. Chop the heart rather more coarsely. Grate or chop the onion finely. Mix with the celery. Add the raisins, grated lemon rind and juice, the crumbs, melted margarine and nuts. If baking separately, put into a dish, cover well with foil, and cook for about 1 hour in a very moderate oven, or 45 minutes in a moderate to moderately hot oven. Do not over-cook; the celery and nuts should retain some of their firm texture.

Vary by adding some chopped pineapple, chopped soaked (but not cooked) dried apricots, or making a more moist stuffing with orange juice. *Serves 8-10*

## Using nut meats ❄❄❄

There are many kinds of nut meat or vegetable protein foods on the market. Most of these have the protein value of lean meat—some are meat-flavoured, and so are ideal to replace meat in savoury dishes.

*Canned nut meat* or protein food is like a round cooked meat loaf when taken from the can. *Serve as steaks or chops:* i.e. slice as thickly as wished, and fry in a little oil or fat, or brush with melted fat or oil and grill for a short time. Serve with tomatoes and mushrooms, or topped with fried eggs.
*Serve as a roasted small joint:* put into a little hot fat in a roasting tin and heat through for about 25 minutes. This can be served with brown sauce, apple or tomato sauce (see the opposite page), with roast potatoes and other vegetables, and with any stuffings normally served with meat or poultry.
*Serve in stews:* make a vegetable stew as page 35, and add the diced nut meat a short time before serving. As the nut meat provides the protein, beans may be omitted from the stew.
*Use in meat patties:* dice raw potato, raw onion, and the nut meat, and use as a filling in vegetarian Cornish pasties; flavour with herbs, seasoning and a little gravy, made with water and yeast extract. Or put the diced meat into a brown sauce, as given opposite, spoon into a pie dish, top with wholemeal pastry, page 67, and bake for about 25-35 minutes in the centre of a hot oven.

*Dehydrated vegetable protein foods* are most useful as a 'stand-by', to use as and when required.

There are many flavourings to choose from.

Before using, the food must be reconstituted with liquid, and most brands need 1 part solid to 2 parts water, i.e. 4 oz. (1 cup) of protein food to 8 oz. (1 cup) water. Simply add the water; if using hot water, wait for about 5 minutes before using the food; if using cold, wait for about 15 minutes. The meat is then like minced meat, with a soft moist texture. It needs heating for a few minutes only before serving.
*Add to curries, sauces, etc.,* and heat for just a few minutes.

On page 53 is a nut meat sauce to serve with pasta, or as a filling for pancakes, etc.

*Cottage pie:* blend the nut meat with fried onions and tomatoes, top with potatoes, and brown.

## Nut meat risotto ✿✿

| Imperial | American |
|---|---|
| 2 oz. peanut butter | ¼ cup peanut butter |
| 2 onions | 2 onions |
| 6 oz. brown rice | ¾ cup brown rice |
| ¾ pint water or vegetable stock | 2 cups water or vegetable stock |
| *bouquet garni* | *bouquet garni* |
| 2-4 oz. mushrooms | ½-1 cup mushrooms |
| 2-3 tomatoes | 2-3 tomatoes |
| sea salt | sea salt |
| cayenne pepper | cayenne pepper |
| 6 oz. diced nut meat | nearly 1 cup diced nut meat |

| to garnish | to garnish |
|---|---|
| chopped parsley | chopped parsley |
| chopped chives | chopped chives |

Heat the peanut butter and cook the chopped onions for a few minutes, then add the rice. Toss in the butter until all the grains are coated with the butter. Add the water or vegetable stock. Bring to the boil, add the *bouquet garni* and cook for about 10 minutes. Put in the whole mushrooms, thickly sliced tomatoes, salt and pepper to taste. Simmer until the rice is almost tender. Add the nut meat. Heat for a few minutes. Pile on to a hot dish and top with the herbs.              *Serves 4-6*

### To vary
If using the dehydrated nut meat or protein food, then you will need 4 oz. (1 cup) of the dried food and 8 oz. (1 cup) water. Allow to stand as instructions on the packet, or information given opposite, then use as above.

## Brown sauce ✿✿

| Imperial | American |
|---|---|
| 1 oz. fat | 2 tablespoons fat |
| 1 oz. wholemeal flour | 3 tablespoons whole-wheat flour |
| ½ pint stock or water | 1⅓ cups stock or water |
| 1 teaspoon yeast extract | 1 teaspoon yeast flavoring extract |

Heat the fat in a pan, stir in the flour, cook gently for several minutes. Gradually add the stock, or water and yeast extract. Bring to the boil, and stir well over a medium heat until the sauce has thickened. This gives a coating consistency; to serve as gravy use about ¾ pint (2 cups) stock, season if wished.    *Serves 4-5*

## Apple sauce ✿✿

| Imperial | American |
|---|---|
| 3 medium sized cooking apples | 3 medium sized baking apples |
| very little water | very little water |
| 2 oz. brown sugar or honey | ¼ cup brown sugar or honey |

Cut the peel from the apples if desired, although this gives an additional flavour to the sauce. Slice the apples and remove the cores; simmer with a little water and sugar until a soft purée.
*Serves 6-8*

### To vary
*Raw apple sauce:* ✿✿ choose dessert apples. Chop the unpeeled fruit in pieces, remove the cores. Put into the liquidiser with a very little water and emulsify until smooth. Add a little honey, if wished. If keeping this sauce for any length of time, substitute a little apple cider vinegar or lemon juice for water, to prevent the sauce becoming brown.

## Tomato sauce ✿✿✿

| Imperial | American |
|---|---|
| 1 large onion | 1 large onion |
| 1 small dessert apple | 1 small dessert apple |
| 1 lb. tomatoes | 1 lb. tomatoes |
| ¼ pint water or vegetable stock | ⅔ cup water or vegetable stock |
| flavouring, see method | flavoring, see method |
| pinch sea salt (optional) | pinch sea salt (optional) |

Peel and grate the onion and grate the apple (unless using a liquidiser, when they may be chopped fairly coarsely). Put into a saucepan with the chopped tomatoes and water or stock. Simmer until a soft purée, add flavouring and salt. If desired, emulsify in the liquidiser. The flavouring of tomato sauce may be adjusted to personal taste:
if you like a *hot sauce*, add a little cayenne pepper and grated fresh horseradish;
if you like a *slightly 'salty' sauce*, add diced celery, celery salt, and brewer's yeast or yeast extract;
if you like a *sweet tomato sauce*, add a little honey or brown sugar or black treacle (molasses).
A tablespoon of wheat germ can be blended with the sauce just before serving. Stir well.

# EGG DISHES

An egg is one of the quickest cooking and most versatile of protein foods. Compared to most foods today, it is extremely inexpensive. Egg yolks add iron, and vitamins A and D, to the diet.

Many egg dishes are spoiled if over-cooked or kept waiting before serving, so time the cooking so that you can 'dish-up' as quickly as possible.

## Basic ways to cook eggs

Use vegetarian margarine or peanut butter (which gives a very pleasant flavour) for cooking the eggs, or use one of the vegetarian fats or corn oil when frying, etc.

*Boiled eggs:* allow about $3\frac{1}{2}$-4 minutes for a lightly-boiled egg. If you wish to shell softly-boiled eggs, cool at once in cold water. Roll the egg round to break the shell; remove the shell very carefully. Serve on top of creamed spinach, lentil purée, onion purée, or a mixture of vegetables.

Hard-boiled eggs need about 10 minutes in boiling water; cool, and crack the shells at once to prevent the dark line forming round the yolk. Serve with various sauces: cheese; onion; parsley; see recipes on pages 48, 74, 76.

*Fried eggs:* fry eggs in oil, peanut butter or vegetarian fat. Serve with vegetables or raw vegetable salads, which add crispness to fried eggs.

*Poached eggs:* break eggs into cups, then slide into steadily boiling water. This can be flavoured with a little yeast extract or sea salt. Poach steadily for about 3 minutes. Serve on top of toast or vegetable mixtures, etc.

*Scrambled eggs:* heat about 1 oz. (2 tablespoons) vegetarian margarine in a pan, add 3-4 beaten eggs blended with seasoning. Cook gently. Grated cheese, bean shoots, diced vegetables may be added.

## Eggs maître d'hôtel ✿✿

| Imperial | American |
|---|---|
| 1 oz. margarine | 2 tablespoons margarine |
| 1 oz. wholemeal flour | 3 tablespoons whole-wheat flour |
| $\frac{1}{2}$ pint milk or soya or plantmilk | $1\frac{1}{3}$ cups milk or soy or plantmilk |
| good pinch sea salt | good pinch sea salt |
| 6 eggs | 6 eggs |
| large sprig parsley, or as much as required | large sprig parsley, or as much as required |

| **to garnish** | **to garnish** |
|---|---|
| paprika | paprika |

Make a sauce with the margarine, flour and milk, season lightly, see page 48. Meanwhile, hard boil the eggs, shell, then cut into thick slices. Chop the parsley and add to the sauce just before serving, or pour the sauce into a hot liquidiser goblet, add parsley and switch on for a few seconds. This retains all the juices and flavour of the herb. Put the eggs into a shallow dish, top with the sauce and paprika. Serve with fresh wholemeal rolls. *Serves 3-4*

## Scrambled eggs italienne ✿✿

| Imperial | American |
|---|---|
| 2 oz. margarine | $\frac{1}{4}$ cup margarine |
| 1 green pepper | 1 green pepper |
| 2 oz. brown rice (cooked until tender, see page 38) | $\frac{1}{3}$ cup brown rice (cooked until tender, see page 38) |
| 3 large tomatoes | 3 large tomatoes |
| 6 eggs | 6 eggs |
| shake of cayenne pepper | shake of cayenne pepper |
| good pinch sea salt | good pinch sea salt |

| **to garnish** | **to garnish** |
|---|---|
| chopped watercress | chopped watercress |

Heat the margarine in a large pan. Cut the green pepper into thin rings, discarding the core and seeds. Add the pepper to the margarine, then stir in the rice and sliced tomatoes, and heat thoroughly. Beat the eggs with the pepper and salt, pour into the rice mixture and stir gently until set. Top with the watercress and serve at once. *Serves 3-4*

## To vary

Use coarse wholemeal crumbs in place of rice.

# Rice stuffed marrow ✿✿

| Imperial | American |
|---|---|
| 1 medium vegetable marrow | 1 medium marrow squash |
| 2 oz. margarine or peanut butter | ¼ cup margarine or peanut butter |

| **for the stuffing** | **for the stuffing** |
|---|---|
| 4 oz. brown rice | ½ cup brown rice |
| ½ pint water or vegetable stock | 1⅓ cups water or vegetable stock |
| 1-2 teaspoons yeast extract | 1-2 teaspoons yeast flavoring extract |
| 1-2 onions | 1-2 onions |
| 1 red pepper | 1 red pepper |
| 4 hard-boiled eggs | 4 hard-cooked eggs |
| 1 teaspoon grated fresh horseradish | 1 teaspoon grated fresh horseradish |

| **for the topping** | **for the topping** |
|---|---|
| 2 oz. wholemeal crumbs | ⅔ cup wholewheat crumbs |

Halve the marrow lengthways, scoop out the seeds. Grease an ovenproof dish with half the margarine or peanut butter. Fill each half with stuffing (see below), top with the crumbs and the rest of the margarine or butter. Bake in the centre of a moderate to moderately hot oven, 375-400°F, Gas Mark 5-6, for 35-40 minutes.
*Serves 5-6*

*To make rice stuffing:* put the rice with the cold water or vegetable stock into a saucepan. Bring to the boil, stir briskly. Cover the pan and lower the heat. Simmer for 15 minutes until all the liquid has been absorbed. This is the easiest way to boil rice. Stir in the yeast extract, then add the finely chopped or grated raw onion, diced pepper, chopped eggs and horseradish. Season with celery salt and cayenne, if wished.

## To vary
The rice stuffing is excellent for stuffing other vegetables such as aubergines, onions, etc. The eggs may be omitted, if wished. Add diced nut meat, or chopped nuts, or grated cheese instead, or increase the amount of vegetables used in the stuffing, i.e. add cooked peas, or chopped raw celery plus some of the chopped young celery leaves.

*Egg and rice savoury:* the stuffing above makes an excellent hot or cold savoury. Prepare as above, blend with yoghourt or a salad dressing (see page 22).

# Eggs in tyrolienne sauce ✿✿✿

| Imperial | American |
|---|---|
| 1 clove of garlic | 1 clove of garlic |
| 1 medium onion | 1 medium onion |
| 4 large tomatoes | 4 large tomatoes |
| 2 oz. margarine or peanut butter | ¼ cup margarine or peanut butter |
| 1-2 teaspoons chopped fresh mixed herbs | 1-2 teaspoons chopped fresh mixed herbs |
| ¼ pint water | ⅔ cup water |
| ½ teaspoon yeast extract | ½ teaspoon yeast flavoring extract |
| 4-6 eggs | 4-6 eggs |

Skin and crush the clove of garlic, peel and chop the onion and tomatoes. Heat the margarine or peanut butter in a frying pan, then cook the vegetables until just soft. Add the herbs, water and yeast extract. Stir together until a purée. Break the eggs carefully into this sauce, poach over a medium heat until just set. Serve at once, either with wholemeal bread or with pasta or rice. *Serves 2-3 as a main dish, or 4-6 as an hors d'oeuvre*

## To vary
Top the dish with grated cheese (Gruyère is an excellent choice) just before serving.

# Eggs in browned butter ✿✿✿

| Imperial | American |
|---|---|
| 2-3 oz. peanut butter | ¼-⅜ cup peanut butter |
| 4 eggs | 4 eggs |

| **to garnish** | **to garnish** |
|---|---|
| chopped parsley or other herbs | chopped parsley or other herbs |

Heat 1 oz. (2 tablespoons) of the butter in a frying pan, fry the eggs until just set. Lift on to a hot dish, keep warm. Put the remainder of the butter into the pan, heat until it becomes a rich brown. Pour over the eggs, top with the parsley or other chopped herbs. Serve at once. (See picture, page 51.)
*Serves 4 as a snack, 2 as a main dish*

## To vary
*Eggs meunière:* ✿✿ fry the eggs as above, keep hot. Brown the rest of the butter with a few capers, a squeeze of lemon juice and 1 tablespoon chopped parsley.

## Eggs with vegetables

Blend 1 or 2 eggs with mashed vegetables to provide extra flavour and food value.

*Stuffed potatoes:* ❋ bake potatoes in their skins. Halve, remove the pulp, mash each potato with 1-2 eggs, a little margarine, seasoning or yeast extract. Add grated cheese, if wished. Pile back into the potato cases and heat.

*Cauliflower polonaise:* ❋❋ hard boil 2 eggs while the cauliflower is cooking. Heat 2 oz. ($\frac{1}{4}$ cup) peanut butter or margarine in a pan, fry a few wholemeal crumbs until crisp, add chopped eggs and a little parsley. Spoon over cauliflower.

## Courgette and tomato bake ❋❋

| Imperial | American |
|---|---|
| about 8 oz. courgettes | about 8 oz. zucchini |
| little sea salt | little sea salt |
| 2 oz. margarine or peanut butter | $\frac{1}{4}$ cup margarine or peanut butter |
| 2 medium onions | 2 medium onions |
| 1 green pepper | 1 green pepper |
| $\frac{1}{4}$ pint dry cider or white wine | $\frac{2}{3}$ cup dry apple cider or white wine |
| 2 teaspoons chopped mixed herbs | 2 teaspoons chopped mixed herbs |
| 8 oz. tomatoes | 8 oz. tomatoes |
| 3-4 hard-boiled eggs | 3-4 hard-cooked eggs |
| 2 oz. soft wholemeal crumbs | $\frac{1}{2}$ cup soft wholewheat crumbs |
| 2 oz. grated Cheddar cheese | $\frac{1}{2}$ cup grated Cheddar cheese |

Wipe the courgettes, but do not peel them. Cut into fairly thin slices. Sprinkle lightly with salt if wished, and leave for about 30 minutes. This draws out the juice and gives a drier result. Fry the sliced courgettes in the hot margarine or butter in a frying pan or shallow saucepan, until golden on both sides. Lift out and put into an ovenproof dish. Peel and chop the onions, dice the green pepper. Remove the core and the seeds. If you like a slightly hot flavour, then retain a few seeds. Put into the frying pan with the cider or white wine and simmer for 10 minutes. Spoon over the courgettes. Add the herbs, the thickly sliced tomatoes, sliced eggs, crumbs and cheese. Put into the centre of a moderate oven, 350-375°F, Gas Mark 4-5, for approximately 30 minutes. *Serves 4*

## Pancakes ❋❋

| Imperial | American |
|---|---|
| 4 oz. wholemeal flour | 1 cup wholewheat flour |
| pinch sea salt | pinch sea salt |
| 1 egg | 1 egg |
| $\frac{1}{2}$ pink milk or soya or plantmilk | $1\frac{1}{3}$ cups milk or soy or plantmilk |

| **to cook** | **to cook** |
|---|---|
| olive or corn or sun-flower seed oil, or vegetarian fat | olive or corn or sun-flower seed oil, or vegetarian fat |

Sieve the flour and salt, add the egg and enough milk to make a thick batter. Beat hard until smooth, then gradually add the rest of the milk. Heat about $\frac{1}{2}$ tablespoon oil in the pan, pour in enough batter to give a very thin coating. You will need to tilt the pan so the batter flows over the bottom. Cook over a fairly high heat for about 2 minutes, until set, then turn and cook on the second side for the same time. Lift on to a hot plate or dish, and keep hot, over a pan of boiling water or in a low oven, while cooking the rest of the pancakes. Add a little oil before cooking each pancake.

### Savoury fillings for pancakes

*Cheese pancakes:* ❋❋ spread each pancake with cheese sauce (page 48) or cottage cheese, then roll, or make a *Cheese pancake gateau:* ❋❋ spread the first pancake with cheese, add a second pancake, more cheese, then a third pancake. Continue like this. Heat gently in the oven if necessary. The cheese may be mixed with chopped vegetables. *Serves 4*

*Vegetable pancakes:* ❋❋ fill each pancake with cooked or raw vegetables, the most suitable are: spinach; tomatoes (including thick tomato sauce, page 43); mixed vegetables as in vegetable stew (page 35). *Serves 4*

### Sweet fillings for pancakes

*Apple raisin pancakes:* ❋ mix grated or finely chopped raw apples with raisins and chopped nuts. Moisten with orange juice, if wished. Put into the pancakes, roll and top with a little brown sugar. *Serves 4-6*

*Yoghourt sundae pancakes:* ❋❋ mix yoghourt with diced fresh fruit. Keep the mixture very cold, or even ice lightly, then put into the very hot pancakes and serve at once. *Serves 4-6*

## Plain omelette ✳✳✳

| Imperial | American |
|---|---|
| 1 oz. margarine | 2 tablespoons margarine |
| 1 teaspoon olive oil | 1 teaspoon olive oil |
| 3-4 eggs | 3-4 eggs |
| pinch sea salt | pinch sea salt |
| shake of cayenne (optional) | shake of cayenne (optional) |
| 1 tablespoon water | 1 tablespoon water |

Heat the margarine and oil in a small omelette pan. The olive oil prevents the eggs 'sticking' in the margarine. Beat the eggs with the salt, cayenne and water. Do not over-beat this type of omelette. Pour into the hot margarine and oil, allow to set for about ½ minute, then tilt the pan and work the omelette, as the sketches below. Fold or roll away from the handle and serve at once. (See picture, page 51.) *Serves 2*

### To vary

*Cheese omelette:* ✳✳ fill with cottage or grated cheese before folding.
*Mushroom omelette:* ✳✳✳ fill with raw sliced mushrooms or cooked mushrooms before folding.
The firm raw mushrooms make a pleasant contrast to the soft egg mixture.
*Spinach omelette mornay:* ✳✳ fill with cooked spinach just before folding, top with grated cheese and put under a hot grill for 1 minute only.
All vegetable mixtures make good fillings for omelettes. They can also be filled with lentil purée, or fingers of fried nut meat (see page 72). Add 1-2 teaspoons wheat germ to the eggs for extra food value, but increase the amount of water slightly so mixture is not too stiff.

With a fork, move the egg away from the sides of the pan. This allows the liquid egg to flow down the sides of the pan. Continue like this

## Soufflé omelette ✳✳✳

The ingredients for a savoury soufflé omelette are the same as the plain omelette, but separate the yolks from the whites. Beat the yolks with the water, etc; whisk the whites until very stiff. Fold the whites into the yolks. Pour into the hot margarine and oil, cook for about 2 minutes. It is difficult to 'work' a soufflé omelette, for the mixture is firm and so very light. Heat the grill as you start to cook the eggs, then put the omelette pan under the grill so you set the eggs from the top; this makes sure the omelette does not take too long to cook. Fill as suggested in the plain omelette recipe.

## Spanish omelette (Tortilla) ✳✳

A Spanish omelette is an excellent way to incorporate a great variety of vegetables into the egg mixture.

| Imperial | American |
|---|---|
| 3 tablespoons olive oil | 3½ tablespoons olive oil |
| 1 medium potato (baked in its jacket or boiled) | 1 medium potato (baked in its jacket or boiled) |
| 1 onion | 1 onion |
| 1 clove of garlic (optional) | 1 clove of garlic (optional) |
| 1 green pepper | 1 green pepper |
| few cooked peas | few cooked peas |
| few raw mushrooms (optional) | few raw mushrooms (optional) |
| 6 eggs | 6 eggs |
| 1 tablespoon chopped parsley | 1 tablespoon chopped parsley |

Heat half the oil in the omelette pan, or a separate pan if preferred. Dice the potato, the peeled onion and garlic, and the green pepper. Heat in the hot oil, then add the peas and sliced mushrooms. Blend with the eggs and parsley. The vegetables give a great deal of flavour, so salt can be omitted here. Heat the rest of the oil in the omelette pan, pour in the egg mixture, cook as the plain omelette, but do not fold before serving. *Serves 2-3*

### To vary

Although not strictly Spanish, bean shoots or other grains can be added to the egg and vegetable mixture.

Cooked sweet corn and peanuts are also very good.

47

# CHEESE DISHES

Cheese is one of the easiest foods to serve. Sprinkle some grated cheese on a soup and immediately it becomes more sustaining and of greater food value. Add cheese to salads and vegetable dishes, or eat bread, cheese and fresh fruit for a complete meal. In addition to having a high protein content, cheese adds calcium, one of the very important minerals for people of all ages.

Cottage cheese is particularly easy to digest and relatively low on calories, so ideal if you wish to lose weight.

The many other cheeses available will give you infinite variety for: salads; sauces; interesting cheese main dishes.

## Leeks in cheese custard ❊❊❊

| Imperial | American |
|---|---|
| 8 small leeks | 8 small leeks |
| little sea salt | little sea salt |
| 2 eggs | 2 eggs |
| 1 level tablespoon wheat germ | 1 level tablespoon wheat germ |
| 4 oz. grated Cheddar cheese | 1 cup grated Cheddar cheese |
| ¼ teaspoon chopped tarragon | ¼ teaspoon chopped tarragon |
| ½ teaspoon chopped sage | ½ teaspoon chopped sage |
| ½ tablespoon chopped parsley | ½ tablespoon chopped parsley |

Cook the leeks in ½ pint (1⅓ cups) boiling salted water until *nearly* tender. Lift out of the vegetable water and save this. Put the leeks into a dish. Beat the eggs, add the wheat germ, leek stock, grated cheese and herbs. Pour over the leeks and bake in the centre of a cool to very moderate oven, 300-325°F, Gas Mark 2-3, for about 45-50 minutes until the custard is lightly set. *Serves 4 as a main dish, or 8 as an hors d'oeuvre*
*Note.* Other vegetables may be used in a similar way—celery, carrots, being particularly good.

## Cheese and vegetable flan ❊

| Imperial for the pastry | American for the pastry |
|---|---|
| 6 oz. wholemeal flour etc., see page 67 | 1½ cups wholewheat flour, etc., see page 67 |

| for the filling | for the filling |
|---|---|
| 2 large carrots | 2 large carrots |
| 4 oz. sliced mushrooms | 1 cup sliced mushrooms |
| small cooked beetroot | small cooked beet |
| 1 green pepper | 1 green pepper |
| 8 oz. cottage cheese | 1 cup cottage cheese |
| 2 oz. grated Cheddar cheese | ½ cup grated Cheddar cheese |
| ¼ pint yoghourt | ⅔ cup yogurt |

Roll out the pastry, line an 8-inch flan ring on an upturned baking tray, and bake 'blind' in the centre of a moderately hot oven, 400°F, Gas Mark 5-6, until crisp and brown. Allow to cool. Grate or shred the carrots into one basin, put the mushrooms into another, the diced beetroot into a third, and the chopped green pepper into a fourth. Divide the cheeses and yoghourt between the basins, and blend well. Arrange the vegetable mixtures in the flan case. *Serves 4*

### To vary
*Egg and vegetable flan:* ❊ mix 2-3 chopped hard-boiled eggs with the cheeses, yoghourt, carrots and pepper. Omit the beetroot and mushrooms.

## Cheese sauce ❊❊❊

| Imperial | American |
|---|---|
| 1 oz. margarine | 2 tablespoons margarine |
| 1 oz. wholemeal flour | 3 tablespoons wholewheat flour |
| ½ pint milk or vegetable stock | 1⅓ cups milk or vegetable stock |
| 2-4 oz. grated Cheddar cheese | ½-1 cup grated Cheddar cheese |
| seasoning (see note at bottom of method) | seasoning (see note at bottom of method) |

Heat the margarine in a pan, add the flour then cook gently for 2-3 minutes, stir well. Blend in the milk or stock (or use a mixture of milk and stock). Bring to the boil, cook until thickened. Add the cheese just before serving, heat gently, season to taste. *Serves 4*

*Note.* Many followers of natural food diets do not add much seasoning, that is why many recipes have very little. Adjust to personal taste.

## Cheese and tomato pie ❋❋

**Imperial**
1 lb. cooked potatoes
2 oz. margarine
6-8 oz. grated Cheddar
  cheese
1 lb. tomatoes
2 teaspoons chopped
  chives
1 tablespoon chopped
  parsley

**American**
1 lb. cooked potatoes
¼ cup margarine
1½-2 cups grated
  Cheddar cheese
1 lb. tomatoes
2 teaspoons chopped
  chives
1 tablespoon chopped
  parsley

Slice the potatoes thinly and put about one-third into a well greased dish. Cover with half the cheese, half the sliced tomatoes and herbs. Put another layer of potatoes over the tomatoes, etc., then the rest of the cheese, tomatoes and herbs. Cover with sliced potatoes and the rest of the margarine. Bake in the centre of a very moderate to moderate oven, 350-375°F, Gas Mark 4-5, for about 40 minutes. Serve with a green salad. *Serves 4-6*

### To vary
This is delicious if 8 oz. (1 cup) cottage cheese blended with ¼ pint (⅔ cup) yoghourt and a little paprika is used instead of Cheddar cheese.

Use sliced Gruyère cheese in place of Cheddar.


## Cheese and mushroom toasts ❋

**Imperial**
1 oz. margarine
4 oz. button
  mushrooms
¼ pint yoghourt
2 hard-boiled eggs
4 oz. grated Cheddar
  cheese
4 slices wholemeal
  bread

**American**
2 tablespoons margarine
just over 1 cup button
  mushrooms
⅔ cup yogurt
2 hard-cooked eggs
1 cup grated Cheddar
  cheese
4 slices wholewheat
  bread

**to garnish**
paprika
chopped parsley

**to garnish**
paprika
chopped parsley

Heat the margarine in a large pan. Add the mushrooms and yoghourt. Heat very gently for about 5 minutes; the mushrooms should still be firm. Add the chopped eggs and cheese, and heat gently. Toast the bread, then pile the mushroom mixture on this. Top with the paprika and parsley. *Serves 4*


## Cheese stuffed peppers ❋❋

**Imperial**
2 large green peppers
1 red pepper
2 medium tomatoes
small piece cucumber
12 oz. grated Cheddar
  cheese
1 tablespoon chopped
  parsley
½ tablespoon lemon juice
about 4 tablespoons
  yoghourt

**American**
2 large green peppers
1 red pepper
2 medium tomatoes
small piece cucumber
3 cups grated Cheddar
  cheese
1 tablespoon chopped
  parsley
½ tablespoon lemon juice
about 5 tablespoons
  yogurt

**to garnish**
lettuce
sliced cucumber

**to garnish**
lettuce
sliced cucumber

Cut a slice from the stalk-end of both green peppers, remove the cores and seeds carefully to keep the peppers a good shape. Dice the flesh of the red pepper finely, discarding core and seeds, and put into a basin. Skin and chop the tomatoes finely; add to red pepper with the finely chopped cucumber, cheese, parsley, lemon juice, and just enough yoghourt to give the consistency of very thick cream. Pack the cheese mixture into the two green peppers, chill for several hours, then slice or halve lengthways. Serve on a bed of lettuce and garnish with sliced cucumber. *Serves 4*

### To vary
If you prefer the green peppers to be slightly softer in texture, blanch for a few minutes in boiling water.


## Fondue ❋

**Imperial**
very little margarine
⅓ pint dry cider or white
  wine
1 lb. Gruyère cheese,
  grated
cubes of wholemeal
  bread

**American**
very little margarine
about 1 cup dry apple
  cider or white wine
4 cups grated Gruyère
  cheese
cubes of wholewheat
  bread

Grease the bottom of a fondue pan with the margarine (rub with a cut clove of garlic before greasing, if wished). Heat the cider or wine in the pan, add the cheese and melt slowly. Stir well until smooth. Keep warm over a gentle heat; at the table dip in the bread with forks.

*Serves about 6*

## Mushroom cups ✿✿

| Imperial | American |
|---|---|
| 12 very thin slices wholemeal bread | 12 very thin slices wholewheat bread |
| about 2 oz. peanut butter or margarine | about ¼ cup peanut butter or margarine |
| 8 oz. chopped mushrooms | 2 cups chopped mushrooms |
| 4 tablespoons water | 5 tablespoons water |
| 1 teaspoon yeast extract | 1 teaspoon flavoring extract |
| 8 oz. cottage cheese | 1 cup cottage cheese |
| 1 tablespoon chopped chives or spring onions | 1 tablespoon chopped chives or scallions |

Roll each slice of bread with a rolling pin to make pliable. Spread one side with some of the butter. Fit the bread, with the buttered side downwards, into 12 patty tins. Melt the rest of the fat and brush over the bread. Bake for 10-15 minutes towards the top of a moderate to moderately hot oven, 375-400°F, Gas Mark 5-6. Meanwhile, simmer mushrooms in the water and yeast extract for about 5 minutes. Cool; blend with cheese and chives or onions. Fill the crisp bread cases with cheese mixture.

*Makes 12*

## Cheese pasties ✿

| Imperial for the pastry | American for the pastry |
|---|---|
| 8 oz. wholemeal flour | 2 cups wholewheat flour |
| pinch sea salt | pinch sea salt |
| 4 oz. vegetarian fat* | ½ cup vegetarian fat* |
| water to mix | water to mix |

| for the filling | for the filling |
|---|---|
| 6 oz. cottage cheese | ¾ cup cottage cheese |
| 6 oz. diced Stilton or Cheddar cheese | nearly 2 cups diced Stilton or Cheddar cheese |
| 2-3 tablespoons yoghourt | 2-3 tablespoons yogurt |
| 1-2 tablespoons chopped parsley | 1-2 tablespoons chopped parsley |

* or use two-thirds fat, one-third cheese

To make the pastry: sieve flour and salt, rub in fat, mix to a rolling consistency with the water. Roll out, cut into 8 rounds, as large as possible. Mix cheeses with enough yoghourt to bind, add parsley. Divide mixture between the rounds. Brush edges of the pastry with water, seal firmly, flute. Bake in the centre of a moderately hot to hot oven, 400-425°F, Gas Mark 6-7, for 20 minutes. *Serves 4*

## Wheat and cheese fingers ✿✿

| Imperial | American |
|---|---|
| 1 teaspoon yeast extract | 1 teaspoon yeast flavoring extract |
| 1 teaspoon water | 1 teaspoon water |
| 8 oz. cottage cheese | 1 cup cottage cheese |
| 2 Shredded Wheat | 2 Shredded Wheat |
| 1 medium carrot | 1 medium carrot |
| 1 tablespoon chopped parsley | 1 tablespoon chopped parsley |

| to garnish | to garnish |
|---|---|
| small lettuce | small lettuce |
| 2 tomatoes | 2 tomatoes |

Put the yeast extract and water into a basin. Add the cottage cheese and mix well. Crumble the wheat and add to the cheese with the grated carrot and parsley. Form into 8 fingers and serve on lettuce. Top with sliced tomatoes.

*Serves 4 as a main dish, 8 as a snack*

**To vary**
*Wheat and nut fingers:* ✿✿ ingredients as above, but use only half the cottage cheese and 2 oz. (½ cup) ground almonds or other ground nuts.

If preferred, omit all the cheese and blend the Shredded Wheat with 4 oz. (1 cup) ground nuts, yeast extract and water, grated carrot and parsley. You may need a little extra water, but keep mixture as dry as possible to avoid spoiling the crispness of the Shredded Wheat.

## Cheese and nut fingers ✿

| Imperial | American |
|---|---|
| 2-3 thick slices of wholemeal bread | 2-3 thick slices of wholewheat bread |
| 8 oz. cream cheese | 1 cup cream cheese |
| little salad dressing, as page 22, or yoghourt | little salad dressing, as page 22, or yogurt |
| about 4 oz. chopped blanched almonds | about 1 cup chopped blanched almonds |

Cut the bread into about 12 fingers. Blend the cream cheese with enough salad dressing or yoghourt to spread easily. Coat all sides of the fingers with a thin layer of cream cheese. Put the chopped nuts on to a sheet of greaseproof paper and turn the cheese coated fingers in this. Press the nuts against the fingers very firmly with a palette knife. *Makes 12*

Other nuts may be substituted for almonds.

Eggs in browned butter, page 45
Omelette, page 47

# PASTA DISHES

Today, a choice of pasta is available in wholemeal flour, and so you can make any of your favourite pasta dishes with this. Wholemeal pasta, like bread, etc., made with wholemeal flour, is very satisfying and has an excellent flavour; it is also another source of protein in the diet.

Never over-cook pasta, it should retain a firm texture and 'nutty' flavour. To test whether the pasta is cooked, press firmly with a fork. When the pasta is adequately cooked it should break when pressed *firmly* against the sides of a pan with a fork.

## Perfect pasta

Allow plenty of water when cooking pasta, i.e. at least 2 pints (5-6 cups) to each 4 oz. pasta. Make sure the water is boiling rapidly when adding the pasta; details of cooking the long spaghetti are below. Allow the pasta to cook for about 5 minutes, then lift in the water with 2 forks to separate the pieces. Cook until tender; this is about 8 minutes for the quick cooking (elbow length) wholemeal pasta, and about 12-15 minutes for the longer type. (See the way to test in the introduction above.) Strain the pasta and serve with the sauce or other accompaniments. If you wish to cook the pasta earlier and do not wish it to become sticky, then rinse under the cold tap. To reheat pasta put into a saucepan of cold water, bring to the boil as quickly as possible, strain and serve.

*To cook long spaghetti:* heat the water in a big saucepan, add a little sea salt if wished. Hold the spaghetti in one hand and lower the ends into the boiling water, allow these to soften. Turn the spaghetti ends so they drop into the water, thus enabling you to lower more of the uncooked spaghetti, continue like this until all the spaghetti lengths are covered with the water, and cook until tender. Lift during cooking as described above.

## Macaroni cheese ❁❁

| Imperial | American |
|---|---|
| 4 oz. short length wholemeal macaroni | ¾ cup short length wholewheat macaroni |
| water to cook | water to cook |
| sea salt (optional) | sea salt (optional) |

| for the sauce | for the sauce |
|---|---|
| 1½ oz. peanut butter or margarine | 3 tablespoons peanut butter or margarine |
| 1½ oz. wholemeal flour | just over ⅓ cup wholewheat flour |
| ¾-1 pint liquid | 2-2⅔ cups liquid |
| seasoning (see method) | seasoning (see method) |
| 6-8 oz. Cheddar cheese, grated | 1½-2 cups grated Cheddar cheese |
| 2-3 tablespoons wholemeal breadcrumbs | 2-3 tablespoons wholewheat breadcrumbs |

Cook the macaroni in the boiling salted water, as described on the left, for about 8 minutes, strain. Heat the peanut butter or margarine in a pan, stir in the flour and cook for several minutes, then gradually add the liquid. If you are browning this under a hot grill, then you can use the smaller quantity of liquid. If you intend to heat the dish in the oven, I would use the larger quantity, since this tends to 'dry out' slightly in the oven. The liquid can be macaroni water if you do not wish to use milk, or soya or plantmilk, or a mixture of macaroni water and milk. Add seasoning if wished. If you do not use much salt or pepper in cooking, then a little yeast extract can be added to the sauce for extra flavour and vitamins. Stir most of the cheese into the sauce. Blend with the drained macaroni, put into an ovenproof dish, top with rest of the cheese and crumbs. Brown under a hot grill, or heat for about 30 minutes above the centre of a moderate to moderately hot oven, 375-400°F, Gas Mark 5-6. *Serves 4-5*

### To vary

*Tomato macaroni cheese:* ❁❁ make the tomato sauce on page 43 (you will need double quantity), add the cheese and macaroni, as the recipe above, top with the remainder of the grated cheese and crumbs and brown as above.

*Macaroni vegetable casserole:* ❁❁ cook the macaroni as recipe above; make vegetable stew as page 35. Blend macaroni and vegetable mixture, top with cheese and crumbs, brown as the recipe above under the grill, so the vegetables do not become over-cooked.

## Vegetarian spaghetti bolognese ✾✾

| Imperial | American |
|---|---|
| 8 oz. wholemeal spaghetti | 8 oz. wholewheat spaghetti |
| water to cook | water to cook |
| sea salt (optional) | sea salt (optional) |

| **for the sauce** | **for the sauce** |
|---|---|
| 2 tablespoons olive or corn oil | nearly 3 tablespoons olive or corn oil |
| 1-2 cloves of garlic | 1-2 cloves of garlic |
| 1-2 onions | 1-2 onions |
| 2 large tomatoes | 2 large tomatoes |
| 2-4 mushrooms (optional) | 2-4 mushrooms (optional) |
| 4 oz. dehydrated nut meat or vegetable protein | 1 cup dehydrated nut meat or vegetable protein |
| 8 fl. oz. water | 1 cup water |
| little white wine | little white wine |
| sea salt | sea salt |
| cayenne pepper | cayenne pepper |

| **to garnish** | **to garnish** |
|---|---|
| chopped parsley | chopped parsley |
| grated cheese | grated cheese |

Cook the spaghetti as described in the left-hand column opposite. The sauce should be started as soon as the spaghetti begins cooking, or can be made before cooking the pasta. Heat the oil in a pan, add the crushed cloves of garlic, finely chopped onions, tomatoes, mushrooms. Meanwhile, blend the nut meat with hot water, allow to stand for about 5 minutes, add to the vegetable mixture and cook for about 5 minutes. Add a little white wine to make a more liquid mixture. Taste, add seasoning, or add a little yeast extract if wished. Nut meats and vegetable proteins are well flavoured, so be sparing with the seasoning. Strain the spaghetti, pile on to a hot dish and top with the sauce, parsley and cheese. Serve with extra grated cheese if required. *Serves 6-8 as an hors d'oeuvre, or 3-4 as a main dish*, excellent with green salad.

## Spaghetti milanaise ✾✾

Cook the spaghetti as the recipe above and serve with the tomato sauce on page 43. You will need double the quantities in the sauce recipe for 8 oz. spaghetti. Serve topped with grated cheese, and hand dishes of grated cheese separately. Choose Cheddar, Gruyère or Parmesan cheese, or for a change top with spoonfuls of cottage cheese, or slices of Camembert cheese. Be sparing with the cheese if slimming.

## Lasagne verdi ✾

| Imperial | American |
|---|---|
| 8 oz. spinach-flavoured lasagne | 8 oz. spinach-flavored lasagne |
| water to cook | water to cook |
| sea salt (optional) | sea salt (optional) |

| **ingredients** *for the bolognese sauce (left)* | **ingredients** *for the bolognese sauce (left)* |
|---|---|
| 4 oz. Ricotta (cream) cheese | ½ cup Ricotta (cream) cheese |
| 4-6 oz. Gruyère cheese | 4-6 oz. Gruyère cheese |
| 2 oz. grated Parmesan cheese | ½ cup grated Parmesan cheese |

Cook the lasagne as described on page 52 (left-hand column) until just tender. Strain, then arrange the long strips of pasta over the edge of the saucepan, as the sketch below. This enables them to 'dry out' and keep their shape. Make the bolognese sauce. Put a layer of lasagne into a casserole, add a little sauce, then some of the cream cheese, thinly sliced Gruyère cheese and a light sprinkling of Parmesan cheese. Fill the dish like this, ending with lasagne, sliced cheese and grated cheese. Do not put the cream cheese on top of the dish as it burns easily. Heat through in the centre of a very moderate oven, 325-350°F, Gas Mark 3-4, for about 35-40 minutes. This dish is very rich in flavour, so serve with a green vegetable or salad. *Serves 4-6*

### To vary

Use the tomato sauce on page 43. If you like a very moist texture make both the bolognese and tomato sauces, cover one layer of lasagne with tomato sauce, the next layer with the bolognese sauce.

Lasagne drying out

## Spaghetti and cheese casserole ✿✿

| Imperial | American |
|---|---|
| 2 oz. margarine | $\frac{1}{4}$ cup margarine |
| 2 large onions | 2 large onions |
| 1 clove of garlic | 1 clove of garlic |
| 4 large tomatoes | 4 large tomatoes |
| 2-4 oz. mushrooms | $\frac{1}{2}$-1 cup mushrooms |
| 1-2 carrots | 1-2 carrots |
| $\frac{1}{4}$ pint white wine or cider | $\frac{2}{3}$ cup white wine or cider |
| seasoning (optional) | seasoning (optional) |
| $\frac{1}{2}$ teaspoon chopped sage | $\frac{1}{2}$ teaspoon chopped sage |
| 2 tablespoons chopped parsley | 2 tablespoons chopped parsley |
| 8 oz. wholemeal spaghetti | 8 oz. wholewheat spaghetti |
| water to cook | water to cook |
| sea salt (optional) | sea salt (optional) |
| 4-6 oz. Cheddar cheese, grated | 1-1$\frac{1}{2}$ cups grated Cheddar cheese |

| to garnish | to garnish |
|---|---|
| fresh sage leaves | fresh sage leaves |

Heat the margarine and fry the finely chopped onions, garlic, tomatoes and mushrooms. Add the coarsely grated carrots, the wine or cider. Season if wished. Simmer for a short time, but do not over-cook, then add the sage and parsley. Meanwhile, cook the spaghetti as the instructions on page 53 (left-hand column). Strain the spaghetti, mix with the vegetable sauce, add the cheese and put into a hot dish, top with several sage leaves. Do not add too much sage as the flavour is very strong. *Serves 8 as an hors d'oeuvre, 3-4 as a main dish*

### To vary
Add a small chopped red chilli pepper (very hot) and/or diced green pepper or red pepper.

## Herbed spaghetti ✿✿

| Imperial | American |
|---|---|
| 8 oz. wholemeal spaghetti | 8 oz. wholewheat spaghetti |
| water to cook | water to cook |
| sea salt (optional) | sea salt (optional) |
| 1-2 oz. margarine | $\frac{1}{8}$-$\frac{1}{4}$ cup margarine |
| 2 tablespoons freshly chopped herbs | 2 tablespoons freshly chopped herbs |

Cook the spaghetti as the instructions on page 53 (left-hand column). Strain, and return to the saucepan with the margarine and herbs, mix well and serve at once. *Serves 3-4 as a main dish*

## Spaghetti and egg bake ✿✿

| Imperial | American |
|---|---|
| 4 oz. wholemeal spaghetti | 4 oz. wholewheat spaghetti |
| water to cook | water to cook |
| sea salt (optional) | sea salt (optional) |
| 2 oz. margarine | $\frac{1}{4}$ cup margarine |
| 1 large onion | 1 large onion |
| 1 tablespoon chopped parsley | 1 tablespoon chopped parsley |
| 4 eggs | 4 eggs |
| seasoning (optional) | seasoning (optional) |

Cook the spaghetti as the instructions on page 53 (left-hand column). Strain, then chop into small pieces. Heat the margarine, fry the sliced onion, add the spaghetti, then parsley, beaten eggs and seasoning. Pour into a shallow casserole, and bake in the centre of a moderate oven, 350-375°F, Gas Mark 4-5, for about 30 minutes, until well risen. *Serves 3-4*

### To vary
Add about 4 oz. (1 cup) grated cheese to the mixture above.

Add about 4 oz. ($\frac{1}{2}$ cup) cooked corn to the mixture above.

## Spaghetti with spiced pepper sauce ✿✿

Make the tomato sauce as page 43, and cook 4 oz. spaghetti as the instructions on page 53 (left-hand column). Add a good pinch of cayenne pepper, a little grated nutmeg and a diced green pepper to the tomato sauce. Put in a few seeds from the pepper to give a hotter flavour. If you enjoy really hot flavours, add a pinch chilli powder and a pinch curry powder. Mix the spaghetti with the sauce, put into a hot shallow casserole, top with poached eggs. *Serves 3-4*

## Crisp fried noodles ✿✿

Cook egg noodles as the instructions for cooking pasta on page 53 (left-hand column). Be very careful they are not over-cooked but are still slightly firm in texture. Rinse under cold water, and spread on a flat dish to dry. Heat a little olive, corn, or sunflower seed oil in a pan, and fry small quantities of the noodles until crisp and golden brown. Drain on absorbent paper and serve hot with savoury dishes.

Wholemeal pasta rings with peanut butter sauce, pages 52 and 75

# REFRESHING DRINKS

key to stars see page 5

The recipes on this, and the next page, cover a wide diversity of drinks. Honey, blended with apple cider vinegar, has become very popular during the last few years. You can buy it ready-prepared from Health Food Stores under the name of Honegar, or you can make your own. This combination of two very important ingredients has been found to help people sleep better if taken at night, also to give relief to sufferers of rheumatism and to provide renewed energy.

Herb teas are not a modern 'fashion'; they have been made for several centuries. I like them ice cold for summer drinks, and hot at night as a soothing bed-time drink.

Fresh fruit juice can be blended with many other ingredients for hot or cold drinks. Where sweetening has not been added you can, of course, add this. Choose honey or brown sugar.

## Honey and apple cider vinegar ✳✳✳

The quantities of honey and vinegar used are a matter of personal taste. I like to blend ½–1 tablespoon honey and ½–1 tablespoon vinegar, but if you like a sweeter taste increase the proportion of honey. Drink first thing in the morning and/or last thing at night.

For a longer drink, mix with ice and cold water, or with very hot water.

## Herb teas ✳✳✳

Peppermint, parsley, lemon thyme, mint are the herbs that give the most refreshing drinks. You may find you enjoy other herbs. Take a small bunch of herbs, wash them, then bruise the leaves slightly (this 'draws out' the flavour better). Put into a teapot or a strong jug and cover with boiling water, just as though you were making ordinary tea. Strain, and top with slices of lemon. Serve hot or cold.

## Maté tea ✳✳✳

Maté tea is a pleasant change from ordinary tea. Prepare like ordinary tea, using about 1 teaspoon tea and ½ pint (1⅓ cups) water per person. Serve with milk or lemon, or flavour with vanilla pod (vanilla bean) or 1-2 cloves. The strained maté tea may be poured over crushed mint leaves, allowed to cool, then served as a refreshing cold drink. Mix with crushed ice if wished.

## Dandelion coffee ✳✳✳

If you would like a change from ordinary coffee serve dandelion coffee. Allow about 1 teaspoon of the coffee and ½ pint (1⅓ cups) water per person. Blend the coffee with the cold water, heat steadily, strain and serve with milk, or as black coffee. This is also very good as iced coffee, strained over crushed ice and topped with natural yoghourt.

## Milk drinks

In many recipes mention has been made of soya or plantmilk. This is an excellent alternative to cow's or goat's milk in cooking, but most people find it less satisfactory as a drink, or added to drinks. If you do not wish to use full-cream milk, substitute skimmed milk in drinks.

## Orange egg nog ✳✳

Put the juice of 1 orange, ¼ pint (⅔ cup) milk, 1 egg and a little crushed ice into the liquidiser. Switch on until blended. Serve in a tall glass, topped with orange slice.          *Serves 1-2*

## Fruit milk shake ✳–✳✳✳

Put a chopped dessert apple, several table-spoons raspberries or strawberries, blackcurrants, etc., or the juice of an orange or lemon, into the liquidiser. Add about ½ pint (1⅓ cups) milk and a little crushed ice. Switch on until blended. Serve at once.     *Serves 2*

## Almond milk shake ✿✿

| Imperial | American |
|---|---|
| 1 tablespoon almonds (blanched if wished) | 1 tablespoon almonds (blanched if wished) |
| 2 teaspoons black treacle | 2 teaspoons molasses |
| 2 teaspoons wheat germ | 2 teaspoons wheat germ |
| about 12 tablespoons milk | 1 cup milk |

Put all the ingredients into the liquidiser. Add crushed ice if wished. Switch on until emulsified. *Serves 1 as a very nutritious and satisfying drink*

## Carob milk drink ✿✿

| Imperial | American |
|---|---|
| 1 tablespoon carob powder | 1 tablespoon carob powder |
| 1 tablespoon honey | 1 tablespoon honey |
| about 12 tablespoons milk—hot or cold | 1 cup milk—hot or cold |

Carob powder comes from a special bean and it gives a pleasant chocolate-like flavour to drinks, etc. It is very easily digested. Put all the ingredients into the liquidiser, switch on until smooth and 'fluffy'. *Serves 1*

## Carrot and raisin milk shake ✿✿

| Imperial | American |
|---|---|
| 1 medium carrot | 1 medium carrot |
| 1 tablespoon raisins | 1 tablespoon raisins |
| about ½ pint milk—hot or cold | about 1⅓ cups milk—hot or cold |

Chop the carrot. Put all the ingredients into the liquidiser. Add a little crushed ice if you require a cold drink.
Switch on until light and 'fluffy'. *Serves 2*

### To vary
Use soda water in place of milk, or orange juice in place of milk.
Add crushed ice and serve cold.

*To make drinks without a liquidiser (blender):* grate or crush ingredients. Whisk in a jug.

## Fruit drinks

These drinks may be served hot or cold. Use soda water for an aerated drink, or mineral water if preferred. Hot fruit drinks make excellent 'night-caps'.

## Apple fizz ✿✿✿

Blend equal quantities of apple juice and soda or mineral water. Serve cold with crushed ice. If preferred, blend very hot water with the apple juice. If you find the flavour lacking in 'bite', add a little fresh lemon juice or apple cider vinegar to taste.

## Orange riser ✿✿✿

Blend fresh orange juice with a little yeast extract or brewer's yeast. At first this unusual blending of fruit juice and yeast may seem 'odd', but it is an excellent start to the day.

### To vary
*Orange and molasses:* ✿✿ blend 1-2 teaspoons black treacle (molasses) with orange juice.

*Orange and honey:* ✿✿ flavour orange juice with honey. Stir 1-2 teaspoons wheat germ into the juice. The orange juice may be heated if preferred but do not allow it to boil, otherwise you destroy most of the vitamin C.

## Cranberry and pineapple ✿

| Imperial | American |
|---|---|
| 1-2 tablespoons fresh cranberries | 1-2 tablespoons fresh cranberries |
| ½ pint hot pineapple juice | 1⅓ cups hot pineapple juice |
| little honey or brown sugar | little honey or brown sugar |

If you are not using a liquidiser, crush the cranberries. Add the hot pineapple juice and honey or brown sugar and mix well. If using a liquidiser, then put all the ingredients into the goblet, switch on until light and 'fluffy'. If preferred, serve cold over crushed ice. *Serves 2*

*Orange or other fruit* juices may be used.

# DESKERTS

Many people feel that puddings and desserts are not necessary in a well balanced diet, but I think a well chosen dessert can 'round off' a meal.

Fresh fruit is the most perfect of all desserts, but if you are watching your weight do not eat too many of the high calorie fruits, i.e. bananas, avocado pears, or dried fruits.

Yoghourt, which is readily available today— or which you can make for yourself, if wished—is a perfect combination with fruit. Natural yoghourt is one of the low calorie desserts too.

When making moulds, etc., I have given the choice of either gelatine or caragheen moss to set the liquid, etc.

## Fresh fruit ❊❊—❊❊❊

Fresh, uncooked, fruit is the perfect dessert. The raw fruit retains the maximum flavour, vitamins and mineral salts. Serve fruit, with the peel on, as often as possible. Wash or wipe it well before eating, particularly in hot weather, when fruit is exposed to flies and dust. Washing also removes any sprays that might have been used on the fruit during growth.

## Cooked fruit ❊❊

Cook fruit as quickly, and for as short a period, as possible. Peel and slice hard fruit, such as apples (or keep the peel on), halve large plums, apricots, etc. Make a syrup of water and pure cane brown sugar, or water and honey. Put prepared fruit into the boiling liquid. Boil for 1-2 minutes only, cover pan tightly, turn off heat and allow the fruit to cook in the steam. In this way you do not spoil the appearance of the fruit, and you also retain the fresh flavour.

*To make a fruit purée:* cook the fruit with the minimum of water and sugar or honey to taste.

## Fresh fruit jelly—with gelatine ❊❊

| Imperial | American |
|---|---|
| 1 pint fresh fruit juice | 2⅔ cups fresh fruit juice |
| brown sugar or honey to taste (optional) | brown sugar or honey to taste (optional) |
| ½ oz. gelatine (or enough to set 1 pint) | 2 envelopes gelatin (or enough to set 2⅔ cups) |

Put most of the fruit juice into a pan with the sugar or honey. Do not add too much sweetening. Soften the gelatine with the remaining cold juice. Stir into the hot liquid, continue stirring until thoroughly dissolved. Pour into a mould, previously rinsed out in cold water, leave to set. Turn out on to a damp dish (which enables you to move the jelly into the centre). To turn out: dip the mould for a few seconds into hot water, invert on to the damp plate.          *Serves 4*

## Fresh fruit jelly—with caragheen moss ❊❊

| Imperial | American |
|---|---|
| 1 pint fresh fruit juice | 2⅔ cups fresh fruit juice |
| brown sugar or honey to taste (optional) | brown sugar or honey to taste (optional) |
| ½ oz. caragheen (Irish) moss | generous tablespoon caragheen moss |

Gelatine is an important protein food, but if you wish to avoid animal products caragheen moss, which is available from Health Food Stores, can be used instead. The moss has valuable iodine properties. Put all the ingredients into a pan, simmer gently for about 8 minutes, then strain through muslin (cheese cloth) and pour into the mould and allow to set.          *Serves 4*

## Apple raisin mould ❊❊

| Imperial | American |
|---|---|
| 1 pint thick apple purée | 2⅔ cups thick apple purée |
| 4 oz. raisins | nearly ⅔ cup raisins |
| ½ oz. gelatine | 2 envelopes gelatin |
| juice 1 lemon | juice 1 lemon |

Heat the apple purée and raisins. Soften gelatine in cold lemon juice, add to apple mixture, stir until dissolved. Put into rinsed mould, allow to set then turn out. This is delicious served chilled with yoghourt, and topped with chopped nuts.          *Serves 4-5*

Pear and hazelnut flan, page 72

## Baked stuffed apples ❋❋

| Imperial | American |
|---|---|
| 4 large cooking apples | 4 large baking apples |
| little brown sugar | little brown sugar |
| little peanut butter or margarine | little peanut butter or margarine |
| about 3 oz. dried fruit | about ½ cup dried fruit |

Core the cooking apples, split the skins round the middle, so the apples will not 'burst' during cooking.

Put into an ovenproof dish, fill the centres with a little sugar, butter or margarine and dried fruit.

Bake for about 1 hour in the centre of a very moderate to moderate oven, 350-375°F, Gas Mark 4-5. Serve hot. *Serves 4*

### To vary
Fill apple centres with brown sugar and shredded fresh or desiccated coconut. Bake as above.

## Orange apples ❋❋❋

| Imperial | American |
|---|---|
| 4 large cooking apples | 4 large baking apples |
| about ¼ pint fresh orange juice | about ⅔ cup fresh orange juice |
| ½-1 teaspoon finely grated orange rind | ½-1 teaspoon finely grated orange rind |

Prepare the apples as above. Put into a baking dish, spoon juice and rind over the fruit. Bake as above. Serve hot or cold. *Serves 4*

### To vary
Blend a little honey with the orange juice.

## Baked oranges ❋❋
Cut the rind from oranges, top with a little margarine and honey.

Bake in a very moderate to moderate oven for about 30 minutes.

## Coconut bananas ❋

Coat peeled bananas with honey and roll in desiccated coconut. Bake for approximately 25 minutes in a very moderate oven. Serve hot or cold.

## Orange and apple bake ❋

| Imperial | American |
|---|---|
| 2 oz. brown sugar | generous ¼ cup brown sugar |
| 1 oz. peanut butter | 2 tablespoons peanut butter |
| 5 medium oranges | 5 medium oranges |
| 2-3 dessert apples | 2-3 dessert apples |

Put the sugar and butter into a pan; stir over a low heat until the sugar has dissolved. Add the juice of 1 orange. Cut the oranges in slices to give rings about ¼ inch in thickness. The oranges are easier to eat if skinned, but the dessert has a more interesting flavour if the skins are left on.

Place a layer of oranges in an ovenproof dish. Core, but do not peel the apples, and cut into rings. Put these over the orange slices, then cover with the rest of the orange slices and the sugar mixture.

Put a piece of foil, or a lid, over the dish and bake in the centre of a moderate oven, 350-375°F, Gas Mark 4-5, for about 35 minutes. Serve hot or cold. *Serves 4-5*

### To vary
Use sliced dessert pears in place of apples.

Use sliced bananas in place of apples.

## Fruit whip ❋❋

| Imperial | American |
|---|---|
| about ¾ pint thick fruit purée, sweetened | about 2 cups thick fruit purée, sweetened |
| 2 egg whites | 2 egg whites |

Allow the purée to thicken, and whisk the egg whites until very stiff.

Fold the egg whites into the fruit purée and chill. *Serves 3-4*

### To vary
*Yoghourt fruit whip:* ❋❋ fold about ¼ pint (⅔ cup) yoghourt into the fruit purée, before the egg whites. *Serves 4*

*Coconut fruit whip:* ❋❋ fold about 2 oz. (⅔ cup) desiccated coconut into the fruit purée, add 1-2 tablespoons dried fruit and the egg whites. Top with toasted coconut. *Serves 4*

*Low calorie whip:* ❋❋❋ use unsweetened fruit purée.

## Making iced desserts

Iced fruit juices or fruit purées make wonderful desserts. They can be frozen in the home freezer, or in the freezing compartment of an ordinary refrigerator, without altering the cold control in any way—as is necessary when making cream ices.

Fruit ices tend to develop small 'splinters' of ice during storage, unless a small quantity of gelatine is used. I do not find caragheen moss has the same ability to prevent this, so if you do not wish to use gelatine, serve fruit ices within 1 or 2 days of making.

The avocado honey ice, right, does not need any gelatine. This is nutritious and sustaining.

## Fruit juice ices ✳✳—✳✳✳

| Imperial | American |
| --- | --- |
| 1 pint fruit juice (see method) | 2⅔ cups fruit juice (see method) |
| 2 teaspoons gelatine | 2 teaspoons gelatin |
| little honey or brown sugar to sweeten | little honey or brown sugar to sweeten |

The fruit juice can be obtained with a juice separator, or by crushing and straining fresh fruit. If using citrus fruit, simmer the thinly pared rind with a little cold water (discard the bitter pith), and add this to the fruit juice for extra flavour and economy. Soften the gelatine in a little cold juice, dissolve over a pan of hot water, remove from heat and add remaining juice. In this way you do not heat the fresh fruit juice and so lose any vitamin content. Add honey or sugar. Do not over-sweeten, for this hinders freezing.

Pour into the freezing tray or utensil; freeze until lightly set. If this becomes too hard, remove from freezer some time before serving. Top with yoghourt and chopped nuts. *Serves 4-5*

**To vary**

*Fruit purée:* use the same method as above, but choose a thick fruit purée (any fruit is delicious) instead of the fruit juice.

*To give a lighter texture* freeze the juice or purée until beginning to ice, remove and blend with 1-3 stiffly whipped egg whites. The more egg whites used the lighter the dessert. (This becomes a fruit sorbet.) If you wish to incorporate the egg yolks, beat these into the fruit juice or fruit purée before freezing.

## Avocado honey ice ✳

| Imperial | American |
| --- | --- |
| 2 large lemons | 2 large lemons |
| 2 ripe avocado pears | 2 ripe avocado pears |
| 4 tablespoons honey | 5 tablespoons honey |

Squeeze the juice from the lemons before cutting the avocado pears, for they discolour very quickly. Halve the pears, remove the pulp from the skins, mash with the lemon juice and honey until very smooth. Spoon into freezing container and freeze as quickly as possible. This is both sustaining and rich in flavour, so will *serve up to 8 people* if accompanied with yoghourt. (See picture, page 23.)

## Fruit and nut cheese cake ✳

| Imperial | American |
| --- | --- |
| 3 eggs | 3 eggs |
| 2 oz. brown sugar | 4 tablespoons (firmly packed) brown sugar |
| 1 lb. cottage cheese | 2 cups cottage cheese |
| 3-4 oz. raisins | about ½ cup raisins |
| 2-3 oz. chopped nuts | ½-¾ cup chopped nuts |
| grated rind 1 lemon | grated rind 1 lemon |
| 2 tablespoons lemon juice | nearly 3 tablespoons lemon juice |
| apples or plums (see method) | apples or plums (see method) |

Beat the eggs and the sugar. Sieve the cheese and add this to the eggs and sugar, then stir in the raisins, nuts, lemon rind and juice. Choose a firm dessert fruit, such as apples or plums. Slice enough apples, or halve enough plums to cover the bottom of a greased 8-9-inch ovenproof flan dish. Put the plums cut side uppermost. Spoon the cheese cake mixture over the top, smooth flat. Bake in the centre of a slow to very moderate oven, 300-325°F, Gas Mark 2-3, for about 1 hour. Allow to cool in the oven, with the heat turned off to prevent the cake wrinkling. The temperature should be checked carefully the first time this is baked, for the cheese cake should be a very pale golden colour when cooked, and should be just firm to the touch. Chill well before serving.

*Serves about 6*

**To vary**

Omit lemon, and add about 3-4 tablespoons yoghourt, to give a soft creamy consistency.

## Caramel bread pudding ❋

| Imperial | American |
|---|---|
| 3 oz. brown sugar | $\frac{1}{3}$ cup brown sugar |
| 2 oz. peanut butter | $\frac{1}{4}$ cup peanut butter |
| $\frac{3}{4}$ pint milk | 2 cups milk |
| 4 slices wholemeal bread | 4 slices wholewheat bread |
| 2 eggs | 2 eggs |

Put the sugar and half the peanut butter into a pan. Stir over a low heat until sugar has dissolved. Take the pan off the heat, allow the sugar to cool slightly so the milk will not curdle. Add the milk and heat gently. Spread the bread with the remainder of the peanut butter. Cut into fingers, put into a pie dish. Add the caramel liquid to the beaten eggs, strain on to the bread and butter. Stand the pie dish in a container of cold water. Bake in the centre of a slow to very moderate oven, 300-325 °F, Gas Mark 2-3, for about 1 hour. Serve hot.      *Serves 4-5*

### To vary
Add 2-3 oz. (about $\frac{1}{2}$ cup) raisins to the bread and butter.

Add about 2 oz. ($\frac{1}{2}$ cup) whole nuts to the bread and butter.

## Fruit crumble ❋

| Imperial | American |
|---|---|
| 1 lb. prepared fruit | 1 lb. prepared fruit |
| brown sugar or honey to taste | brown sugar or honey to taste |

| for the crumble | for the crumble |
|---|---|
| 4 oz. wholemeal flour | 1 cup wholewheat flour |
| 2 oz. peanut butter or margarine | $\frac{1}{4}$ cup peanut butter or margarine |
| 2-3 oz. brown sugar | $\frac{1}{4}$-$\frac{3}{8}$ cup brown sugar |

Put the fruit into a pie dish with the sugar or honey to sweeten. Use a little water with very firm or under-ripe fruit. Cook hard fruit for about 15 minutes, until beginning to soften. Do not cook soft fruit. Put the flour into a bowl, rub in the peanut butter or margarine, add the sugar. Sprinkle over the top of the fruit and bake in the centre of a very moderate to moderate oven, 350-375 °F, Gas Mark 4-5, for 30-35 minutes, until crisp and golden brown.      *Serves 4-5*

## Cranberry-raisin pie ❋

| Imperial for the pastry | American for the pastry |
|---|---|
| 8 oz. wholemeal flour | 2 cups wholewheat flour |
| pinch sea salt | pinch sea salt |
| 4 oz. margarine | $\frac{1}{2}$ cup margarine |
| 2 teaspoons brown sugar | 2 teaspoons brown sugar |
| 1 egg yolk | 1 egg yolk |
| water to mix | water to mix |

| for the filling | for the filling |
|---|---|
| 8 oz. cranberries | 1 cup cranberries |
| 6 oz. raisins | nearly 1 cup raisins |
| 4-6 oz. brown sugar | generous $\frac{1}{2}$-$\frac{3}{4}$ cup brown sugar |
| 1 tablespoon wholemeal flour | 1 tablespoon wholewheat flour |

| to glaze | to glaze |
|---|---|
| 1 egg white | 1 egg white |

Sieve the flour and salt. Rub in the margarine until the mixture looks like fine breadcrumbs. Add the sugar, egg yolk and enough water to bind. Roll out half the pastry and line a 7-8-inch pie plate. Mix the cranberries with all the other ingredients for the filling. Put over the pastry. Brush the edges of the pastry with water. Roll out the rest of the pastry. Cover the filling, seal and neaten the edges. Press together firmly. Brush the pastry with egg white. Bake in the centre of a moderately hot to hot oven, 400-425 °F, Gas Mark 5-6, for about 20 minutes, then lower the heat to moderate and cook for a further 15-20 minutes. Serve hot or cold.      *Serves 4-6*

### To vary
Use sliced apples, halved apricots, plums, etc., instead of cranberries. Cranberries are very 'sharp', so need more sugar than other fruit.

## More fruit pies

The above recipe gives a dessert with pastry above and below the fruit. In America this is known as a fruit pie, in Britain we usually call it a fruit tart.

The same quantity of pastry will cover the fruit in a deep-dish pie.

Put 1-1$\frac{1}{2}$ lb. fruit into a 2 pint (1$\frac{1}{2}$ quart) pie dish, add a little water and sugar or honey to taste. Cover with the pastry, bake as above.

Wholemeal bread, pages 64, 65 and 66

# BAKING WITH WHOLEMEAL FLOUR

Although modern additives in Britain have produced a white bread of greater food value than in the past, it must be accepted that wholemeal stoneground flour, used in baking bread, cakes, etc., is more satisfying in every way and contains the *natural* food values.

If you have never made your own bread you may imagine it is a troublesome and lengthy process. This is *not* the case. Yeast bread dough needs time to rise (or 'prove') but you do not have to handle the dough while it is 'proving'; so can continue with other tasks and simply deal with the bread when necessary.

I have given you two recipes for basic wholemeal bread. In the first recipe the dough is sufficiently firm to knead in the usual way. In the second recipe, you make a dough that is too soft to knead and one that produces a very light loaf. Try both of them, for they make a very pleasant change. I give the amount for making one loaf only, so you may experiment with a relatively small quantity of flour, but home-made wholemeal bread keeps so well that I suggest you do make larger quantities. Increase the water, etc., in proportion but not the yeast. You need $\frac{1}{2}$ oz. fresh yeast for 1 lb. flour, but only 1 oz. yeast for 3 lb. flour. Use fresh yeast where possible. When this is not available substitute dried yeast. You need half the quantity, i.e. 1 oz. fresh yeast means $\frac{1}{2}$ oz. (1 tablespoon) dried yeast (1 15g package active dry yeast). Put the amount of warm liquid and sugar given in the recipe for fresh yeast into a basin. Sprinkle the dried yeast on top, leave for 10 minutes, mix together, then continue as fresh yeast.

In recipes that state 'white flour' add a little more liquid if using wholemeal (finely milled wholewheat) flour, and bake for a few minutes longer.

The recipes in this book are for wholemeal (wholewheat) flour (this is 100% whole wheat), or for wheatmeal flour, which is 80-90% extraction and gives a slightly lighter result in cakes.

Sifting aerates the flour—if coarsely ground, some of the bran may separate, and it should, of course, be added back.

## Success in baking bread

In order to ensure the success of your bread there are some points I would like to emphasise:

### Temperature for handling dough, etc.

Keep the bowl, baking tins, etc., comfortably warm. Make sure the water is only warm (about 98-100°F). Do not put the dough into a *hot* place to 'prove'; *near* the cooker, in the airing cupboard or just at room temperature are ideal.

### Temperature for baking

This should be in a hot oven, so the yeast is quickly 'killed', reduce the heat during cooking (see the recipe, page 65).

### Handling the dough

As already explained, the dough is kneaded in the first recipe, but in the second recipe you can check whether sufficiently handled. Press the dough with a lightly-floured finger and if the impression remains the dough needs longer kneading. When the impression comes out you have kneaded for a long enough period, so stop, for over-handling does *not* improve the bread.

### To test when cooked

Bake until the bread seems well baked. Remove from the tins or baking tray. Invert on to a tea-cloth on the palm of your hand, or a wire cooling tray. Tap the bottom of the bread very firmly. If it sounds 'hollow' the bread is cooked. If it is not cooked, return to the oven for a short period and test again.

### To cool and store bread

Let the bread cool on a wire cooling rack. When *quite cold* wrap in foil, or put into a bread drawer or container *away from* cakes, biscuits or pastry.

### To freshen the bread

As already stated, wholemeal bread keeps well for some days, but *if* it has become stale then warm in the oven for a short time. If you do not wish to over-crisp the crust, wrap in foil.

## Ingredients to use

Your choice of ingredients can add to the successful result of your bread-baking, as well as adding extra flavour and health-giving ingredients.

The choice of flour and yeast have been discussed opposite, but here are some of the other ingredients that are important:

**Fat:** neither recipe gives fat, but you can add up to ½ tablespoon corn or sunflower seed oil to the other ingredients to give a loaf that is a little more moist in texture.

**Flavourings, etc:** nuts, fruit, etc., all add interest to special breads and there are a number of recipe suggestions on page 67.

**Toppings:** a sprinkling of poppy seeds, cracked wheat (crush wheat grains with a rolling pin to give the cracked wheat topping), or rolled oats, may be put on to the bread before baking to give an attractive topping.

**Enriched bread:** soya flour (an excellent source of protein) and wheat germ (which gives vitamins) not only add texture but a delicious flavour to the bread. You may use both together, or just one or the other. I use 1 oz. soya flour to each 1 lb. wholemeal (stoneground) flour and about 2 tablespoons wheat germ.

You will need to prepare your own wheat germ. Put about a cupful of washed wheat grains (which you buy from the Health Food Stores) into a basin. Cover with cold water and allow to soak for about 12 hours. Drain and spread on a large tray or dish with a little warm water on the dish. Cover with a cloth or thick muslin spread over a large sieve or cake rack, and leave for about 3 days. Add enough warm water daily, or twice daily, to moisten the dish. Store in a screw-topped jar. You may like to prepare larger quantities for use in other recipes (see page 67).

**Salt:** the amount of salt can vary according to personal taste. I find I need *less* salt with wholemeal than with white flour, as the flour itself gives natural flavour. Choose sea salt, which possesses traces of valuable natural iodine and other minerals.

**Sugar or sweetening:** use dark Barbados sugar, black treacle (molasses) or honey.

## Wholemeal bread (1) ❄❄❄

| Imperial | American |
|---|---|
| 1 lb. wholemeal flour | 4 cups wholewheat flour |
| up to 1 teaspoon sea salt | up to 1 teaspoon sea salt |
| barely ½ oz. yeast | barely ½ oz. yeast |
| 1 teaspoon brown sugar | 1 teaspoon brown sugar |
| generous ½ pint tepid water | almost 1½ cups tepid water |
| 1 oz. margarine or 1 tablespoon oil (optional) | 2 tablespoons margarine or generous 1 tablespoon oil (optional) |

Blend the flour and salt in a large bowl. Cream the yeast with the sugar, then add most of the liquid. Sprinkle a little flour over the top of the yeast liquid. Stand in a warm place for about 15 minutes until the surface is covered with bubbles. Add the yeast liquid to the flour and salt, blend well, then add any extra liquid to make a soft elastic dough that can be kneaded. The margarine or oil gives a more moist loaf. Rub the margarine into the flour before adding the yeast liquid, or add the oil to the flour, then add the yeast liquid. Knead until the mark of your finger comes out of the dough. Either put the dough back into the mixing bowl and cover with a cloth, or put into a greased large polythene bag (remember it will rise until double its original size, so leave plenty of space). Leave in a warm place for about 1 hour, then knead the dough again until back to its original size. Form into the shaped loaf desired. If making into a tin loaf knead the dough into a neat oblong, fold into three, so it fits a well greased warmed loaf tin, as the picture on page 63. If forming the dough into a loaf, put on to a lightly greased warm flat baking tray or sheet. Allow the loaf to 'prove' (rise) in a warm place for about 20 minutes, then bake for approximately 35 minutes in the centre of a hot oven, 425-450°F, Gas Mark 6-7. Reduce the heat after 20 minutes. Set at moderate to moderately hot. This makes sure the outside of the loaf does not become too brown and hard before the centre is cooked. To test the loaf, turn out of the tin or lift from the flat baking tray or sheet. Turn the loaf upside down, knock the base with your knuckles. The loaf is cooked when it has a hollow sound.

Black treacle (molasses) can be used in place of sugar in the recipe; this gives an excellent colour as well as flavour to the loaf. Honey is another alternative to the sugar.

## Wholemeal bread (2) ❀❀

This recipe for bread is very similar to the one on the previous page. The three differences are:
a) the liquid is increased to give a sticky dough that is beaten, rather than kneaded;
b) the margarine or oil is omitted;
c) the dough is not 'proved' in bulk.
Prepare the yeast mixture, using a generous ½ pint (about 1½ cups) liquid with the yeast, etc. Add this to the flour and salt, then add enough extra tepid water to give a sticky dough. Beat hard with a wooden spoon, until the mixture is smooth and elastic.

As the dough is softer, you achieve a better shaped loaf if it is put into a tin, rather than forming into a loaf on a flat baking sheet or tray. Leave in the tin in a warm place for about 20 minutes until the dough has increased in size by about one-third.

Bake as before. Due to the extra liquid you generally need an extra 5 minutes baking time. Test as page 65.

### To vary
Add wheat germ as described on pages 64 and 65. Put about 1 tablespoon with the flour.

Top the loaf with cracked wheat as in the picture on page 63, or use poppy seeds as a topping.

Use half wholemeal (wholewheat) and half white flour to make a brown loaf. This should be made as recipe (1), and you will need just about ½ pint (1⅓ cups) liquid; the dough should be soft and elastic but easy to knead.

*Milk loaf:* use milk or plantmilk to mix the dough instead of water.

*Rich bread:* use 1 or 2 eggs and milk to mix the dough. If using 1 egg, omit about 2 tablespoons liquid. If using 2 eggs, then omit about 4 tablespoons liquid (5 American tablespoons).

Soya flour enriches bread. I find that if you use 1-2 oz. (¼-½ cup) soya flour to each 1 lb. (4 cups) wholemeal (wholewheat) flour you have both a nutritious loaf and excellent flavour.

**To store bread :** well made wholemeal bread keeps for up to 1 week. Cool, then store in a drawer, bread crock or in a tin, but away from cakes, biscuits, etc.

Or wrap the bread well and freeze.

## Making rolls ❀❀

Choose either of the bread recipes, (1) or (2). The former (page 65) gives a firm crusted roll, the second a very soft textured roll. Prepare the dough as the recipe selected. If using recipe (1) allow dough to 'prove', form into about 12-16 rolls. Put on to well greased, warmed baking trays or sheets. Allow to 'prove' for 10-15 minutes. Bake for about 10 minutes towards the top of a hot oven, see temperature for bread. If using recipe (2) beat the dough until soft and elastic. Grease and warm deep patty tins, put the dough in these or form into rather soft, flat rounds, rather like a Scottish 'bap' or American Hamburger roll. Brush with a little milk or egg and sprinkle poppy seeds or cracked wheat on top. 'Prove' for 10-15 minutes. Bake above the centre of a hot oven for approximately 12 minutes. Cool on a wire tray.

## Baking powder rolls and bread ❀❀

| Imperial | American |
|---|---|
| 1 lb. self-raising wholemeal flour, or plain flour with 4 teaspoons baking powder<br>pinch sea salt<br>water, or milk and water to mix | 4 cups wholewheat flour sifted with 1½ tablespoons double-acting baking powder, or use all-purpose flour with 4 teaspoons double-acting baking powder<br>pinch sea salt<br>water, or milk and water to mix |

Sieve the flour and salt. Add water, or milk and water, to make a fairly soft dough, but one you can handle. Knead lightly until smooth, form into a loaf or about 12-16 rolls. Bake the loaf as the bread on page 65. Bake rolls for 10-12 minutes towards the top of a hot oven. Baking powder bread does not keep as well as yeast bread. A small knob of margarine or a little oil can be added to give a more moist texture.

### To vary
*Making scones:* ❀ use the recipe above, but rub 2-3 oz. (¼-⅜ cup) margarine into 1 lb. (4 cups) flour. Add 2-3 oz. (about ⅓ cup) moist brown sugar, or 2-3 tablespoons honey or treacle (molasses), to the rubbed-in mixture together with a little dried fruit. Bind with milk to give a soft rolling consistency. Roll out to ½-¾ inch in thickness. Put on baking trays, brush with milk, bake for 10-12 minutes towards the top of a hot oven. *Makes 20 scones*

## Fruit breads

Dried fruit may be added to the yeast breads, pages 65 and 66. Use about 4-6 oz. (up to 1 cup loosely-filled) to each 1 lb. (4 cups) flour. There are many interesting and easy-to-make recipes for fruit breads, several are given below.

## Prune bread ❀

**Imperial**
¼ pint milk plus 4 table-spoons water, or water
8 oz prunes
12 oz. self-raising wholemeal flour
4 oz. moist brown sugar
4 oz. nuts
3 oz. margarine or vegetarian fat
2 eggs

**American**
1 cup milk and water, or water
8 oz. prunes
3 cups wholewheat flour sifted with 3-4 teaspoons double-acting baking powder
generous ½ cup moist brown sugar
1 cup nuts
6 tablespoons margarine or vegetarian shortening
2 eggs

Heat the milk and water. Chop the prunes with scissors and put into the liquid. Cover the pan. If the prunes are very dry, leave for 1 hour, if moist for about 20 minutes only. Sieve the flour, add the sugar and coarsely chopped nuts. Melt the margarine or fat. Blend the prunes and liquid, then the melted margarine or fat with the flour, etc., and stir well. Lastly, add the eggs. Line a 2 lb. loaf tin with greased greaseproof paper. Spoon the mixture into the tin, flatten on top. Bake in the centre of a very moderate oven, 325-350°F, Gas Mark 3-4 for a total cooking time of 1¼-1½ hours. Look at the loaf at the end of an hour, and reduce the temperature slightly if becoming too brown. Test by pressing very firmly on top. Turn out carefully and cool on a wire tray. Plain flour with 3 teaspoons baking powder could be used.

### To vary
*Date loaf:* use chopped dates in place of prunes. Put dates into warm liquid for 10 minutes.
*Malt loaf:* add 3 tablespoons powdered malt to the flour, etc. The simplest way to obtain malt is to use one of the malt drink powders.
*Mixed fruit loaf:* use mixed fruit in recipe. Add this to flour, reduce liquid by 2 tablespoons.
*Eggless loaf:* omit the eggs in the recipe above, use 1 tablespoon apple cider vinegar and 2 (nearly 3 tablespoons) extra liquid. Other ingredients as the prune loaf, or variations above.

## Wholemeal pastry ❀

**Imperial**
8 oz. wholemeal flour
pinch sea salt
4 oz. margarine or vegetarian fat
water to mix

**American**
2 cups wholewheat, or all-purpose flour
pinch sea salt
½ cup margarine or vegetarian shortening
water to mix

Blend or sieve the flour and salt. Rub in the margarine or fat, until mixture is like fine breadcrumbs. Add sufficient water to make the dough into a rolling consistency. If you have not previously used wholemeal (wholewheat) flour for pastry, you will find it absorbs more liquid than white flour. Use as individual recipes.

### To vary
To give a lighter texture pastry, use half wholemeal (wholewheat) flour and half white (all-purpose) flour.

*Hazelnut pastry:* used in the menu on page 72. Use ½ oz. (1 tablespoon) *less* margarine or fat, and add 1 oz. (¼ cup) finely chopped or ground hazelnuts. Other nuts may be used instead, and about 1 oz. (¼ cup) brown sugar can be added.

*Cheese pastry:* the margarine or fat can be reduced to 3 oz. (6 tablespoons) but if you keep the original amount, above, you have a richer pastry. Mix a little celery salt and pinch of cayenne pepper with the flour. Rub the margarine or fat into the flour until like fine breadcrumbs. Add 2-3 oz. (½-¾ cup) finely grated Cheddar or Parmesan cheese. Bind with water, or an egg yolk and water.

## Nut cake ✿

| Imperial | American |
|---|---|
| 4 oz. margarine | $\frac{1}{2}$ cup margarine |
| 4 oz. moist brown sugar | generous $\frac{1}{2}$ cup moist brown sugar |
| 2 eggs | 2 eggs |
| 4 oz. self-raising wheatmeal flour* or plain flour and 1 level teaspoon baking powder | 1 cup all-purpose or wheatmeal flour* sifted with 1 teaspoon double-acting baking powder |
| 3 oz. ground nuts | $\frac{3}{4}$ cup ground nuts |
| 1 tablespoon milk or water | 1 tablespoon milk or water |

* I have suggested wheatmeal flour in this recipe as it gives a slightly lighter texture. Wholemeal (finely milled wholewheat) flour can be used if wished.

Cream the margarine and sugar until soft. Gradually blend in the beaten eggs. Add the sieved flour, or flour and baking powder, then the nuts and the milk or water. Grease and flour a 7-inch cake tin, put in the mixture. Bake for 1 hour in the centre of a very moderate oven, 325°F, Gas Mark 3. Do not use a hotter oven than this. Test by pressing gently, the cake is done when firm to the touch.

*Makes about 8 slices*

### To vary
This mixture makes a delicious steamed pudding: cook for $1\frac{1}{4}$ hours over rapidly boiling water. Serve with cooked apricots or other fruit.

## Fruit cake ✿

| Imperial | American |
|---|---|
| 4 oz. margarine | $\frac{1}{2}$ cup margarine |
| 4 oz. moist brown sugar | generous $\frac{1}{2}$ cup moist brown sugar |
| 1 tablespoon treacle | 1 tablespoon molasses |
| 2 eggs | 2 eggs |
| 6 oz. self-raising wheatmeal flour* or plain flour and $1\frac{1}{2}$ level teaspoons baking powder | $1\frac{1}{2}$ cups all-purpose, or wheatmeal flour* sifted with $1\frac{1}{2}$ teaspoons double-acting baking powder |
| 12 oz. mixed dried fruit | 2 cups loosely packed mixed dried fruit |

* see comment about wheatmeal flour on left.

Cream the margarine, sugar and treacle until soft and light. Beat the eggs, then beat gradually into the creamed mixture. Sieve the flour or flour and baking powder, fold into the eggs, etc., then add the fruit. Grease and flour a 7-inch cake tin. Put in the mixture, smooth flat on top. Bake in the centre of a cool to very moderate oven, 300-325°F, Gas Mark 2-3, for $1\frac{1}{4}$-$1\frac{1}{2}$ hours until firm to the touch.

### To vary
Add 2-3 oz. ($\frac{1}{2}$-$\frac{3}{4}$ cup) chopped nuts to the above cake, or flavour with $\frac{1}{2}$-1 teaspoon mixed spice.

*Malt cake:* add 1-2 tablespoons powdered malt to flour. See comments under malt loaf, page 67.

## Peanut cookies ✿

| Imperial | American |
|---|---|
| 3 oz. margarine | 6 tablespoons margarine |
| 2 oz. moist brown sugar | generous $\frac{1}{4}$ cup moist brown sugar |
| 4 oz. self-raising wholemeal or wheatmeal flour | 1 cup wholewheat or wheatmeal flour sifted with 1 teaspoon double-acting baking powder |
| 3 oz. shelled peanuts | $\frac{3}{8}$ cup shelled peanuts |

Cream margarine and sugar. Add flour and peanuts, knead well to blend, then form into balls. Put on well oiled baking trays, allowing space for them to spread out. Bake in the centre of a very moderate oven, 325-350°F, Gas Mark 3-4, for 15 minutes. Cool on the trays. *Makes 12-15.* Or use plain flour with 1 level teaspoon baking powder: other nuts in place of peanuts.

## Fruit muffins ✿

| Imperial | American |
|---|---|
| 8 oz. wholemeal flour | 2 cups wholewheat flour |
| 3 teaspoons baking powder | 3 teaspoons double-acting baking powder |
| pinch sea salt | pinch sea salt |
| 2 oz. moist brown sugar | $\frac{1}{4}$ cup moist brown sugar |
| 2 eggs | 2 eggs |
| $\frac{1}{4}$ pint milk and 4 tablespoons water | $\frac{2}{3}$ cup milk and 4 tablespoons water |
| 2-3 oz. raisins | nearly $\frac{1}{2}$ cup raisins |

Sieve or mix the dry ingredients together. Add eggs, liquid and raisins. Well oil some deep patty (muffin) tins. Spoon the mixture into the tins and bake towards the top of a moderately hot oven, 375-400°F, Gas Mark 5-6, for 15 minutes. *Makes 12-15*

# Sponge cake ❈

**Imperial**
3 oz. margarine
3 oz. brown sugar
2 large eggs
4 oz. self-raising
   wheatmeal flour*
   or plain flour and
   1 level teaspoon
   baking powder
1 tablespoon warm
   water

**American**
6 tablespoons margarine
nearly ½ cup brown sugar
2 large eggs
1 cup all-purpose, or
   wheatmeal flour*
   sifted with 1 teaspoon
   double-acting baking
   powder
1 generous tablespoon
   warm water

*see comment on page 68, column 1.

Cream the margarine and sugar until soft. Gradually add the well beaten eggs, then fold in the sieved flour, or flour and baking powder, and the water. Oil and flour one 8-inch deep sandwich tin. Bake for 25-30 minutes just above the centre of a moderate oven, 350-375°F, Gas Mark 4-5, until firm to the touch. Turn out carefully, and when cold split and sandwich with fresh fruit purée. *Makes 8-10 slices*

*Note.* The amount of margarine should not be increased, but 4 oz. moist brown sugar (generous ½ cup) may be used.

## To vary
Use this as a basis for a steamed pudding: steam for 1-1¼ hours over rapidly boiling water.

# Butterfly cakes ❈

**Imperial**
**ingredients** as sponge
   cake above, but
   *omit water*

**American**
**ingredients** as sponge
   cake above, but
   *omit water*

**for the filling**
2 oz. margarine
2 tablespoons
   honey
2 oz. chopped nuts

**for the filling**
¼ cup margarine
nearly 3 tablespoons
   honey
½ cup chopped nuts

Make the mixture as sponge cake above. Oil and flour fairly deep patty (muffin) tins. Spoon the mixture into the tins, bake for approximately 12 minutes towards the top of a moderately hot oven, 375-400°F, Gas Mark 5-6. Cool, cut the top off each cake. Halve the slices to form 'wings'. Beat the margarine and honey together, add the nuts. Spread the mixture over the top of the cakes, press the 'wings' in position.
*Makes approximately 12 cakes*

# To make a flan

Choose any of the pastries, page 67.

Pastry made with 4 oz. (1 cup) flour, etc., makes a 7-inch flan if not too deep, or the pastry required not too thick. You need 5-6 oz. (1¼-1½ cups) flour, etc., for a similar 8-inch flan, or up to 8 oz. (2 cups) flour, etc., for a really deep 8-9-inch flan. Make the pastry. Put the flan ring on an upturned baking tray. Support the pastry over a rolling pin. Lower into the flan ring. Press down at the base with your fingers. To give a neat top edge, either cut away the surplus pastry or press the rolling pin over the top edges. This 'cuts' the extra pastry away.

*To bake blind:* put greased or oiled greaseproof paper (with the greasy side downwards) into the flan case, fill with dried beans, crusts of bread, etc. Bake in the centre of a hot oven (cheese, sweet and nut pastries need a moderately hot oven) for approximately 15-20 minutes, until the pastry has set. Lift the paper, etc., from the flan case, lower the heat slightly. Continue cooking for 5-10 minutes. Individual flans with fillings (e.g. page 72) may require slightly different baking times, etc.

# Some fillings for flans

**Savoury fillings**
Use cheese or plain pastry, recipes page 67. Bake the flan as the recipe above, fill with:
a) grated raw carrots, blended with thick cheese sauce or onion sauce (pages 48, 74);
b) fried diced nut meat, blended with thick tomato sauce (page 43);
c) cottage cheese, blended with a little sour-sweet dressing (page 22), chopped chives, chopped cucumber and chopped tomatoes. Serve cold, or put into the oven to warm for a short time.

**Sweet fillings**
Use plain, nut or sweet pastry, recipes page 67. Bake the flan as the recipe above, fill with:
a) honey, blended with grated lemon rind and juice to taste, and chopped nuts;
b) sliced fruit, topped with a little honey;
c) chopped fresh pineapple, topped with mince-meat, recipe page 75.

# CHOOSING MENUS

On this and the next few pages are suggestions for menus throughout the year.
They make use of many recipes in the book, together with additional suggestions.
You will find the menus marked at the heading with bold stars, these denote the calorie content of the *whole menu*.

If there are ✿✿✿ this means you can eat generous quantities of all the dishes.

Other menus are marked ✿✿, which indicates that you must take only reasonable helpings.

If the menu is marked ✿, beware!! the dishes are high in calories, and you must be very sparing in eating portions if you wish to lose weight.

Obviously by omitting a course, or substituting another dish, you can alter the rating of the meal to suit your own requirements.

SUMMER meals should make use of the great variety of salad ingredients and fruit available.

SPRING menus are fairly low in calories, for all too often one eats more carbohydrates in the cold weather.

AUTUMN and WINTER menus include warming soups and sustaining protein dishes, as well as a generous amount of citrus fruits. The vitamin content in the latter helps 'build up' resistance to the all too prevalent 'flu and colds of damp or wintry weather.

# summer menus

## Nut cutlets with ✿✿ creamed beetroot
## Mushrooms on toast

Make the cutlets as the variation on page 78. Serve hot or cold.
*Creamed beetroot:* grate cooked beetroots coarsely, put into a pan with a small knob of margarine and add sufficient yoghourt to moisten. Heat gently, top with chopped parsley.
Serve cooked mushrooms on crisp wholemeal (wholewheat) toast.

## Orange juice ✿
## New potato mould with green beans
## Avocado honey ice

Orange juice is very pleasant if flavoured with a few mint leaves.
*Potato mould:* scrape about $1\frac{1}{4}$ lb. new potatoes, or cook with their skins. Slice potatoes thinly, also 8-12 oz. onions and 12 oz.-1 lb. tomatoes. Arrange layers of vegetables in a well margarined tin, beginning and ending with potatoes. Season, if wished, and brush each layer with melted margarine. Bake for about $1\frac{1}{4}$ hours in the centre of a moderate oven, 350-375°F, Gas Mark 4-5. Turn out, serve with cheese sauce, if desired. The ice recipe is on page 61.

## Almond rice roast ✿
## with green salad
## Berry nut cake

Follow directions for roast on page 40. Make nut cake as recipe on page 70; when cold, split and fill with crushed raspberries, or other berry fruit. Top with more berries and serve with yoghourt.

## Apricot and ✽✽ cucumber soup

## Cheese and vegetable flan

## Blackcurrant froth

Make and chill the soup as page 11. Prepare the flan, the recipe is on page 48. Choose a colourful selection of young summer vegetables for the filling.

*Blackcurrant froth:* use 1 lb. blackcurrants, crush and sieve. Add a little honey to sweeten. Whisk 2 egg whites until stiff, fold into the blackcurrant purée. Freeze for about 40 minutes until lightly frosted. Spoon into glasses, top with yoghourt.

## Spinach juice ✽✽✽ cocktail

## Poached eggs with tomato salad

## Gooseberry sorbet

Make cocktail as page 30. Use summer greens if spinach is not available (often difficult to obtain in hot weather). If you do not have equipment for making vegetable cocktails, start with fruit juice, or tomato salad, and serve lightly cooked green vegetable with the eggs.

*Gooseberry sorbet:* cook gooseberries with minimum of water, sweeten to taste. Sieve or emulsify. Freeze for $\frac{1}{2}$ hour, mix with 2-3 stiffly whisked egg whites. Continue freezing. Use yolks for Hollandaise sauce.

## Savoury courgettes ✽✽ with new potatoes

## Berry and cottage cheese cups

*Savoury courgettes:* slit lengthways, and cook in a steamer over boiling water until tender. If preferred, cook in a small quantity of peanut butter in a pan with a tightly fitting lid. Top with lightly scrambled eggs, flavoured with fresh herbs and enriched with a little wheat germ and brewer's yeast.

Sweeten cottage cheese with honey or brown sugar, and serve with fruit.

## Carrot cocktail ✽✽✽

## Summer cauliflower with Hollandaise sauce

## Strawberry orange baskets

This is an excellent time of year to make the cocktail (page 30), as carrots and parsley are young and full of flavour. Cook cauliflower (or broccoli), top with sauce.

*Hollandaise sauce:* (enough for 4 people) whisk 3 egg yolks with $\frac{1}{2}$-1 tablespoon lemon juice and seasoning in a basin over *hot* water until thick. Gradually whisk in 2-3 oz. ($\frac{1}{4}$-$\frac{3}{8}$ cup) softened margarine.

Halve the oranges, remove pulp, mix with strawberries. Put back into orange cases.

## Chilled tomato soup ✽✽

## Cheese and nut salad

## Berry fruit salad

Make and chill the tomato soup as page 14. Top with yoghourt and freshly chopped herbs. As tomatoes have been included in the first course, base the salad on grated Cheddar cheese, lettuce, watercress, grated young raw carrots, turnip and diced young cooked beetroot. Top with mayonnaise (page 22) and chopped walnuts.

Slice fresh strawberries, mix with raw redcurrants, blackcurrants. Moisten with a little orange juice.

## Melon cocktail ✽✽

## Herb omelette with summer vegetables

## Summer pudding

*Melon cocktail:* halve a medium melon, remove seeds, dice the pulp. Blend juice of 1 or 2 oranges with a little chopped green ginger (when available) or powdered ginger. Pour over diced melon and chill.

Mix freshly chopped herbs with the eggs. Make omelettes as page 47.

*Summer pudding:* line a basin with thin slices of wholemeal (wholewheat) bread. Simmer about 1-1$\frac{1}{4}$ lb. raspberries, or raspberries and redcurrants, in the minimum of water and a little brown sugar or honey. Pour into the bread-lined basin. Top with more bread. Put a weight on top. Leave for 12-24 hours. Turn out and serve.

# autumn menus

### Beetroot soup ✻
### Bean casserole
### Apple flan

Make the beetroot soup as
page 12, top with chopped
nuts. Follow the casserole
recipe on page 32, which uses
haricot (navy) beans, but use
1 lb. sliced runner beans
instead. Do not cook the beans
as haricot beans, just put into
boiling water, cook for
5 minutes, drain, and use in
the casserole as the recipe.
Make a flan as page 69. Fill
with apple purée, blended with
raisins.

### Date and orange ✻✻
### cocktail
### Fried nut meat with
### mixed salad
### Plum sundaes

*Date and orange cocktail:* put
a few stoned dates with
orange juice into the liquidiser
(blender) goblet, and emulsify
until smooth. This is fairly
thick, so serve with a spoon.
If you have no liquidiser, chop
the dates finely and allow to
stand in orange juice.
*Fried nut meat:* cut slices of
nut meat, dip in a little milk,
or use plantmilk and roll in
flour or oatmeal. Fry in hot oil
until crisp and brown.
*Plum sundaes:* halve ripe
dessert plums, put into glasses
with a little honey. Top with
yoghourt and grated nutmeg.

### Celery cocktail ✻✻
### Wheat roast with
### baked savoury
### tomatoes and roast
### potatoes
### Autumn fruit salad

The recipe for the cocktail is
on page 30 and the wheat
roast on page 37.
*Savoury tomatoes:* halve large
tomatoes, spread with a very
little margarine, blended with
yeast extract. Bake for about
10 minutes. Scrub the potatoes,
do not peel, roast in hot
vegetarian fat for about
50 minutes.
Blend sliced apples, pears,
plums, etc. Moisten with
orange juice.

### Clear mushroom ✻✻
### soup
### Cheese Waldorf salad
### Pear and hazelnut flan

Soup and salad recipes pages
13, 20.
The *Pear and hazelnut flan*
(using 8 oz. flour) serves
6 people, so if catering for 6
prepare more salad and soup.
Make hazelnut version of flan
(page 69). Bake 'blind' for
10 minutes. Arrange 6-8 halved
peeled pears in case. Blend
$\frac{1}{4}$ pint ($\frac{2}{3}$ cup) cream or cream
substitute with 2 oz. ($\frac{1}{4}$ cup)
brown sugar, 2 oz. ($\frac{1}{2}$ cup)
hazelnuts and 1-2 tablespoons
wheat germ. Pour over pears,
bake in very moderate oven for
30 minutes (picture page 59).

### Citrus cocktail ✿✿
### Lasagne verdi
### Blackberry and apple mould

*Citrus cocktail:* mix segments of grapefruit, orange and tangerine together. Moisten with lemon juice blended with honey. The recipe for lasagne is on page 53.
*Blackberry and apple mould:* make a sweetened purée with cooked blackberries and apples. To each 1¼ pints (about 3½ cups) allow 1 envelope of gelatine (enough to set 1 pint — 2⅔ cups). Soften the gelatine in a little cold purée. Heat the rest of the purée and dissolve the gelatine in this. Serve with yoghourt flavoured with grated nutmeg or cinnamon.

### Raw mushroom ✿✿ salad
### Stuffed cauliflower, jacket potatoes
### Plum cheese cake

*Salad:* slice well washed button mushrooms, toss in the Yoghourt 1000-Island dressing (page 22). Top with freshly chopped herbs and serve on a bed of watercress. Stuffed cauliflower recipe, page 28. Use *firm* dessert plums in the recipe on page 61.
Extra plums may be simmered with brown sugar or honey, to serve as a sauce with the cheese cake. Damsons are another excellent fruit sauce with this cheese cake. As they have so many stones, simmer and sieve before using.

### Tomato onion soup ✿✿
### Lentil loaf with buttered cabbage
### Cider pears

Use the recipe for tomato soup on page 14, but increase the onions from 1 to 4. The lentil loaf is on page 32.
*Buttered cabbage:* shred the cabbage finely; heat 2 oz. (¼ cup) peanut butter in a large pan; put in cabbage and toss for 4-5 minutes in the heated butter until hot, but still crisp.
*Cider pears:* simmer halved firm pears in cider until tender. Add honey or treacle (molasses) to taste. If preferred, omit the cider, and use orange juice or orange and lemon juice instead.

### Tomato fondue ✿✿
### Lentil and cheese cutlets with macédoine of vegetables
### Fresh fruit shortcake

Fondue recipe on page 29, and cutlets on page 78.
*Macédoine of vegetables:* dice mixed vegetables; boil until tender, toss in margarine with mixed herbs to taste.
*Fresh fruit shortcake:* cream 4 oz. (½ cup) peanut butter and 4 oz. (generous ½ cup) brown sugar until soft. Add 1 egg and 6 oz. (1½ cups) self-raising wholemeal (wholewheat) flour (or plain flour and 1½ teaspoons baking powder). Divide between two 7-inch greased and floured sandwich tins. Bake for 15-20 minutes in moderate oven. Cool, sandwich and top with autumn fruits.

### Apple soup ✿✿
### Salad niçoise
### Cheese and wholemeal (wholewheat) rolls

*Apple soup:* simmer chopped apples with water and a little brown sugar. Flavour with lemon juice, or cider vinegar, to give a 'sharp' flavour. Sieve or emulsify. Serve hot or cold. The soup should be fairly thin, but it can be thickened with fine wholemeal (wholewheat) or rye crumbs.
*Salad niçoise:* line a bowl with crisp lettuce, pile in mixed cooked green beans, sliced tomatoes, sliced cooked new potatoes, olives, diced cucumber. Top with mayonnaise (page 22). Cottage cheese and mixed herbs can be blended with mayonnaise for an interesting dressing, or add little cayenne pepper and celery salt.

### Les crudites ✿✿✿
### Cottage cheese and tomato bake
### Orange apples

You can arrange a most interesting salad in the early autumn months (see page 18).
*Cottage cheese and tomato bake:* choose 8 *large* tomatoes, halve, remove the pulp; chop finely and blend with about 8 oz. (1 cup) cottage cheese, 1-2 tablespoons chopped chives or spring onions (scallions) and 1-2 tablespoons diced cucumber; season lightly, pack mixture into the tomato cases and bake for 10 minutes in a moderately hot oven.
The Orange apple recipe is on page 60. If using early autumn windfalls, cut into thick slices and cook for about 20 minutes only.

# winter
# menus

key to stars see page 70

## Egg cutlets ✽✽
## Celery cole slaw
## Stuffed baked apples

The cutlets recipe is on page 78.
*Celery cole slaw:* blend shredded cabbage, chopped celery, chopped nuts and raisins with mayonnaise; flavour with a generous amount of celery salt, chopped parsley and chopped chives.
The recipe for stuffed baked apples is on page 60. An interesting version is to crush fresh blackberries, mix with brown sugar, honey or treacle (molasses) and put into the apple centres before cooking.

## Chestnut soup ✽✽
## Celeriac bake
## Coconut bananas

The recipes for the soup and coconut bananas are given on pages 12 and 60.
*Celeriac bake:* buy one celeriac. This is a delicious vegetable, looking like an unattractive turnip, but with the flavour of celery (often called celery root). Peel, cut into slices about $\frac{1}{4}$ inch thick, then divide into fingers. Put in water with a teaspoon apple cider vinegar, to retain the white colour. Lift out, and use as the recipe for courgette and tomato bake on page 46: omit courgettes. The celeriac retains much of its firm texture in the bake.

## Parsley and lemon ✽✽
## cocktail
## Mushroom burgers with jacket potatoes
## Cheese dreams

The cocktail recipe is on page 30, the burgers on page 28.
*Cheese dreams:* cut slices of wholemeal (wholewheat) bread and spread with peanut butter or margarine. Sandwich with yeast extract and cheese. Use sliced Cheddar or other firm cheese, or cottage cheese or sliced Camembert, etc. Cut the sandwiches into fingers, dip in beaten egg or egg and milk. Fry in a little olive or corn oil, until crisp and golden brown on either side. Serve hot.

## Fresh grapefruit ✽✽
## Grilled nut meat with onion sauce
## Raisin pancakes

*Grilled nut meat:* cut nut meat into slices. Brush with melted margarine or peanut butter. Grill until hot and golden on one side; turn and continue cooking. Serve with grilled tomatoes.
*Onion sauce:* chop 2 large onions, simmer in $\frac{1}{2}$ pint ($1\frac{1}{3}$ cups) water until just tender. Do not over-cook: it is much nicer when the onions are slightly firm. Blend nearly 1 oz. (2 tablespoons only) of flour with a little water, or milk or plantmilk. Add to the liquid and cook until thickened. Add yeast extract to taste, and a small knob peanut butter or margarine. Fill pancakes (page 46) with raisins blended with honey.

## Apple and avocado ✳ salad

## Lentil curry

## Rhubarb-raisin pie

The avocado salad is on page 21. Choose avocado pears that are just ripe and a fairly 'sharp' eating apple. The lentil curry is given on page 33. The pie is an adaptation of the recipe on page 62, but substitute chopped rhubarb for cranberries. As rhubarb is less sour than the berries, reduce the amount of sugar to about half that given in the recipe. Other winter fruits to use are shelled chestnuts and sliced apples or pears.

## Stuffed nut roast ✳✳ with apple sauce

## Fruit whip

Use the recipe for peanut bake on page 41. Choose any stuffing; the following is one of the best with a nut roast. *Sage and onion stuffing:* chop and boil 2 large onions in the minimum of water for 5 minutes. Strain, keep the stock. Add 2 oz. ($\frac{2}{3}$ cup) soft breadcrumbs, 1-2 teaspoons chopped fresh sage, 1 oz. (2 tablespoons) margarine, plus a little seasoning and stock to moisten. Put half the roast on an oiled baking dish, top with the stuffing, the rest of the roast, and cook as recipe, page 41, allowing extra 10 minutes. Serve with brown and apple sauces, page 43. Fruit whip is on page 60. Apples and cranberries are excellent in this.

## Onion soup ✳

## Cheese with apple cole slaw

## Pancakes with orange sauce

Follow recipes for soup, page 13; the apple cole slaw, page 20; and pancakes on page 46.
*Orange sauce:* grate the rind from 2 large oranges, simmer with about $\frac{1}{4}$ pint ($\frac{2}{3}$ cup) water and 2 tablespoons honey, for about 5 minutes. Cover the pan so the liquid does not evaporate. Add the diced orange segments. Heat for 1 minute but no longer, to preserve the vitamin C.

## Pasta rings with ✳✳ peanut butter sauce and salad

## Ogen baskets

Cook 8 oz. wholemeal pasta rings in boiling salted water until soft. Drain and toss in chopped fresh herbs.
*Peanut butter sauce:* meanwhile, heat 2 oz. ($\frac{1}{4}$ cup) peanut butter in a pan, stir in 1 oz. (3 tablespoons) wholemeal (wholewheat) flour, gradually add $\frac{3}{4}$ pint (2 cups) milk or pasta liquid. Bring sauce to the boil, cook, stirring well, until thickened. Flavour with yeast extract and cayenne pepper. Pour over the pasta, top with chopped parsley and sliced tomatoes (picture page 55).
*Ogen baskets:* halve 2 large Ogen melons, or cut tops off 4 small ones. Remove seeds and fill with fresh fruit (picture page 31).

## Boston baked beans ✳✳

## Sprouts and chestnuts

## Fresh fruit

*Boston baked beans:* soak 12 oz.-1 lb. haricot beans (2 cups navy beans) overnight in water to cover, then strain. Fill a casserole with the beans, 2-3 sliced onions, 2-3 tablespoons treacle (molasses), blended with $\frac{1}{2}$ pint (1$\frac{1}{3}$ cups) liquid used to soak the beans, a little mustard, sea salt, pepper and 1-2 oz. ($\frac{1}{8}$-$\frac{1}{4}$ cup) peanut butter. If you eat meat, add 12 oz. diced fat pork and omit the butter, see picture page 27. Cover the casserole, cook in a very slow oven for 5-6 hours, stir from time to time. This serves 6-8. Cook sprouts and shelled chestnuts in *separate pans*, then mix together and serve.

## Lentil soup ✳

## Leeks in cheese custard

## Mincemeat apples

Recipe for soup, page 15; leek dish, page 48; stuffed apples, page 60—use mincemeat filling.
*Mincemeat:* blend 1 lb. (almost 2$\frac{1}{2}$ cups) mixed dried fruit, 4 oz. (good $\frac{1}{2}$ cup) brown sugar, 4 oz. ($\frac{1}{2}$ cup) melted margarine, 1 large grated apple, 4 oz. (1 cup) nuts, chopped coarsely; add $\frac{1}{2}$-1 teaspoon each of allspice, cinnamon, grated nutmeg. Moisten with 4 tablespoons orange juice or whisky (to keep the preserve). Cover, store in a dry place. The mincemeat keeps less well with orange juice. A little orange or lemon rind may be added.

# spring menus

## Tomato juice ❋❋
## Peas bonne femme with cucumber salad
## Fresh fruit

Flavour tomato juice with a little rosemary and tarragon, to make a change.
*Peas bonne femme:* cook about 2 lb. peas until tender. Meanwhile, slice and fry 4 oz. (1 cup) mushrooms in 2 oz. ($\frac{1}{4}$ cup) margarine or peanut butter. Strain the peas, mix with the mushrooms, top with chopped mint and chives.
*Cucumber salad:* slice the cucumber thinly, season lightly and add a small quantity of apple cider vinegar to flavour.

## Tomato salad ❋❋
## Baked aubergines and new potatoes
## Fresh fruit jelly

*Salad:* slice 4-6 tomatoes, top with a little cider vinegar, sea salt, celery salt and cayenne. Serve with watercress and garnish with chopped chives and parsley.
*Baked aubergines:* make a cheese sauce with 1 oz. (2 tablespoons) margarine, 1 oz. (3 tablespoons) wholemeal (wholewheat) flour, $\frac{3}{4}$ pint (2 cups) milk or soya or plantmilk. Season lightly, and add 4 oz. (1 cup) grated cheese. Wash, dry and thinly slice 2 aubergines (egg plants). Put into a shallow dish. Top with the sauce, bake in the centre of a moderate oven, 350-375°F, Gas Mark 4-5, for 40 minutes. Follow jelly recipe on page 58.

## Grilled grapefruit ❋
## Whole grain soufflé and cauliflower salad
## Cheese and nut fingers

*Grilled grapefruit:* spread honey over the top of halved, prepared grapefruit. Put under the grill until the honey begins to 'bubble'. Serve at once, so the vitamins are not lost. Divide the cauliflower into flowerets (sprigs), coat with mayonnaise, as page 22, top with chopped chives. Serve with watercress.
Cheese and nut fingers are on page 50.

## Apple fizz ❋❋
## Broad beans with parsley sauce and green salad
## Fresh fruit jelly

The apple fizz on page 57 is an excellent start to a meal.
*Broad beans:* cook both the pods and insides of the broad (lima) beans. The beans may be cooked whole when small, or the pods removed, sliced and cooked separately as a sliced green bean, then the beans cooked in another pan.
*Parsley sauce:* heat 1 oz. (2 tablespoons) margarine in a pan, stir in 1 oz. (3 tablespoons) wholemeal flour, gradually add $\frac{1}{2}$ pint (1$\frac{1}{3}$ cups) milk or plantmilk. Bring to the boil, cook until thickened, stirring well. Add seasoning and 1-2 tablespoons chopped parsley.

## Lemon appetiser ✲

## Spaghetti with spiced pepper sauce and nuts

## Sponge cake filled with fruit

*Lemon appetiser:* squeeze the juice from 3 or 4 lemons. Put the juice and 1-2 tablespoons honey in the liquidiser (blender) goblet. Add 2 unwhisked egg whites, and a little crushed ice. Switch on until light and fluffy. This serves 4 people.
The spaghetti recipe is on page 54. Serve on a hot dish, top with a generous amount of coarsely chopped nuts.
Make the sponge cake on page 69. Fill with fresh fruit.

## Les crudites ✲✲

## Rice stuffed marrow with tomatoes

## Cherry flan

Spring time is excellent for serving a selection of crisp salad ingredients as an hors d'oeuvre. Include baby spring onions (scallions), radishes, etc., see page 18.
Marrows (zucchinis) are young and tender. Use the recipe on page 45, but you may need several smaller vegetables at this time of the year, rather than a large marrow (squash).
Make a flan as page 69, fill with raw or slightly cooked cherries. Coat in honey, then top with yoghourt.

## Springtime soup ✲✲

## Cheeseburgers with green salad

## Rhubarb and dates

The soup recipe is on page 10.
*Cheeseburgers:* blend 8 oz. (1 cup) cottage cheese, 4 oz. (1 cup) grated Cheddar cheese, 2 oz. ($\frac{2}{3}$ cup) wholemeal (wholewheat) crumbs, 1 tablespoon chopped parsley, 1 tablespoon chopped chives or spring onions (scallions), 2 oz. ($\frac{1}{2}$ cup) chopped nuts. Bind with an egg, and season if wished. Form into 8 flat cakes. Either fry in hot oil or grill. Cook chopped dates with rhubarb and honey.

## Mixed salads with ✲✲ cheese scones

## Fresh fruit

This is the kind of quick meal that enables you to enjoy a warm spring day. Include plenty of nuts and citrus fruits with your salad. Add cooked early beans, peas, for extra protein.
*Cheese scones:* sieve a good shake celery salt and cayenne pepper with 8 oz. (2 cups) self-raising wholemeal flour (wholewheat flour with baking powder). Rub in 1 oz. (2 tablespoons) margarine, add 2 oz. ($\frac{1}{2}$ cup) grated Cheddar cheese. Bind to a soft rolling consistency with milk or plantmilk. Roll out to about $\frac{3}{4}$ inch in thickness, put on baking trays. Brush with milk or egg. Bake for 10-12 minutes towards the top of a hot oven.

## Green pea soup ✲

## Nut pilaff with cole slaw

## Redcurrant kissel

Late spring is an ideal time to make the soup, for the peas and pods are so tender, they can both be used, see page 15. The nut pilaff is on page 40, and the cole slaw on page 20.
*Redcurrant kissel:* simmer 1 lb. redcurrants with a little honey to sweeten, and water to provide plenty of juice. Sieve or emulsify if wished. Blend in 1 oz. (3 tablespoons) wholemeal (wholewheat) flour with a little juice and cook, stirring well, until thickened. Allow to cool. The dessert is rather like a soup. Serve with yoghourt. Use rhubarb or other fruits if too early for redcurrants.

## Cucumber and ✲✲ orange salad

## Lentil loaf with potatoes Anna

## Fresh fruit sundaes

The salad is on page 18 and the lentil loaf on page 32.
*Potatoes Anna:* scrape new or peel old potatoes (or simply wash, and leave the skins on). Cut into wafer-thin slices. The slicing attachment shown on page 19 is ideal for this. Brush a cake tin with a little corn oil or melted margarine. Put in a layer of potato, brush with oil or margarine, season lightly. Continue to fill tin with neat layers of potato. Bake in a very moderate oven, as lentil loaf, but allow about $1\frac{1}{4}$ hours. Turn out, top with chopped herbs.
Use mixed spring fruits, layer with fruit ices (as page 61) and yoghourt.

# PACKED MEALS

key to stars see page 5

It is comparatively easy to take a meal of health foods, for they need so little preparation. Wholemeal (wholewheat) bread with cheese, or eggs and salad, and fresh fruit gives a splendid meal for any time of the year. If the weather is very cold, add a hot soup carried in a vacuum flask. If the weather is very hot, cold fruit juices may be chilled and kept at a low temperature in the flask. The recipes on this page are suitable for packed meals.

## Stuffed cheese loaf ❄❄

| Imperial | American |
| --- | --- |
| 1 small wholemeal loaf | 1 small wholewheat loaf |
| 2 oz. margarine | ¼ cup margarine |
| 1 onion | 1 onion |
| 1½ oz. wholemeal flour | 6 tablespoons whole-wheat flour |
| ½ pint milk or soya or plantmilk, or vegetable stock | 1⅔ cups milk or soy or plantmilk, or vegetable stock |
| 8 oz. grated Cheddar cheese | 2 cups grated Cheddar cheese |
| 1 green pepper | 1 green pepper |
| 2-3 oz. peanuts or other nuts | about ½ cup peanuts or other nuts |
| seasoning (optional) | seasoning (optional) |

Cut a slice from the loaf, remove the crumb, break half into tiny pieces, use the rest for stuffings, etc. Heat the margarine, add the finely chopped or grated onion, cook for several minutes, blend in the flour, and proceed as cheese sauce (page 48), but this is a rather thicker mixture. Add the diced green pepper, nuts and crumbs. Season if desired, pack back into the loaf 'case'. Top with the slice of bread, wrap in foil, heat for about 10 minutes in the oven, then serve hot. To serve cold, chill loaf *then* slice and wrap in foil; serve with salad. The loaf may be stuffed with cottage cheese mixed with chopped nuts, green or red peppers, spring onions and cucumber. *Serves about 6 as a snack, 3-4 as a main dish*

## Egg cutlets ❄❄

| Imperial | American |
| --- | --- |
| 6 hard-boiled eggs | 6 hard-cooked eggs |
| 1 egg | 1 egg |
| 2 oz. wholemeal crumbs | ⅔ cup wholewheat crumbs |
| 1 tablespoon chopped spring onions or chives | 1 tablespoon chopped scallions or chives |
| 1 teaspoon chopped parsley | 1 teaspoon chopped parsley |
| 1 tablespoon wheat germ | 1 tablespoon wheat germ |
| 1-2 teaspoons brewer's yeast | 1-2 teaspoons brewer's yeast |

| **to coat** | **to coat** |
| --- | --- |
| 1 egg | 1 egg |
| 2 tablespoons fine wholemeal crumbs | 2 tablespoons fine wholewheat crumbs |

| **to fry** | **to fry** |
| --- | --- |
| 2-3 tablespoons corn oil | 2-3 tablespoons corn oil |

Shell and chop the eggs, blend with the whole egg, crumbs, spring onions, parsley, wheat germ and yeast. If omitting the yeast, add a little sea salt. Form into 8 cutlet shapes, coat in the beaten egg and crumbs, then fry until crisp and golden brown. Do not over-cook for the cutlets should retain their firm texture. Drain well on absorbent paper. Serve hot with tomato sauce, page 43, or cold with salad. Wrap in foil or polythene to carry. *Serves 4*

### To vary
*Lentil and egg cutlets:* ❄❄ use cooked lentil purée in place of crumbs. If the lentil purée is sufficiently sticky to bind the mixture together, omit the egg. If the lentil purée is rather thick, then retain the egg; otherwise the cutlets are too dry.

*Cheese and egg cutlets:* ❄❄ add 2 oz. (½ cup) grated cheese. The crumbs can be omitted if wished, although the mixture is a little difficult to bind without them.

*Tomato and egg cutlets:* ❄❄ use 2 skinned chopped tomatoes to bind, instead of the egg.

*Lentil and cheese cutlets:* ❄ use cooked lentil purée in place of crumbs. Omit 3 of the eggs, use 4 oz. (1 cup) grated cheese instead.

*Nut cutlets:* ❄❄ omit the eggs entirely and use at least 8 oz. (1 cup) nuts. Chop the nuts coarsely (unless you find them indigestible, then grind finely), mix with other ingredients.

# INDEX